RAND NATIONAL DEFENSE RESEARCH INSTITUTE

The Military Spouse Education and Career Opportunities Program

Recommendations for an Internal Monitoring System

Gabriella C. Gonzalez, Laura L. Miller, Thomas E. Trail

Prepared for the Office of the Deputy Assistant Secretary of Defense

Approved for public release; distribution unlimited

For more information on this publication, visit www.rand.org/t/RR1013

Library of Congress Cataloging-in-Publication Data is available for this publication.
ISBN: 978-0-8330-9594-7

Published by the RAND Corporation, Santa Monica, Calif.
© Copyright 2016 RAND Corporation
RAND® is a registered trademark.

Cover: *TheaDesign/iStock*.

Preface

The Office of the Deputy Assistant Secretary of Defense for Military Community and Family Policy sought assistance from the RAND Corporation to assess whether and how initiatives under the Department of Defense's Spouse Education and Career Opportunities (SECO) program address objectives in supporting the education and employment of military spouses. These initiatives include the My Career Advancement Account Scholarship, career counseling services available through the SECO Call Center, the Military Spouse Employment Partnership, and Department of Defense State Liaison Office initiatives to expand unemployment compensation eligibility for trailing military spouses and to secure cross-state endorsements of professional certifications and licenses. This report recommends a system by which SECO staff can conduct internal monitoring of the portfolio of these efforts as a way to document and track progress of early outcomes, suggest midterm corrections, and lay important groundwork for more in-depth investigation of whether longer-term objectives are being met. This report describes the logic of the program, key performance indicators, and the steps in building and utilizing the monitoring system.

The research reported in this document is part of a larger RAND project to support the monitoring and evaluation of Military Community and Family Policy's SECO program, which reviewed existing SECO metrics and data sources, as well as analytic methods of previous research, to determine whether and how they might be appropriate to employ in an evaluation of SECO efforts. A related RAND report emerging from this project analyzes responses to the 2012 Active Duty

Spouse Survey: *Advancing the Careers of Military Spouses: An Assessment of Education and Employment Goals and Barriers Facing Military Spouses Eligible for MyCAA*, by Esther M. Friedman, Laura L. Miller, and Sarah Evans (2015). A separate RAND effort to evaluate one of the SECO initiatives is described in *Evaluation of the Military Spouse Employment Partnership: Progress Report on First Stage of Analysis*, by Gabriella C. Gonzalez, Luke J. Matthews, Marek N. Posard, Parisa Roshan, and Shirley M. Ross (2015).

This research should be of interest to policymakers responsible for programs or oversight of programs supporting military spouse quality of life and to scholars who study military spouse issues. It also should interest scholars who study program evaluation, as well as education and employment benefit programs more generally.

This research was sponsored by the Office of the Deputy Assistant Secretary of Defense for Military Community and Family Policy and conducted within the Forces and Resources Policy Center of the RAND National Defense Research Institute, a federally funded research and development center sponsored by the Office of the Secretary of Defense, the Joint Staff, the Unified Combatant Commands, the Navy, the Marine Corps, the defense agencies, and the defense Intelligence Community.

For more information on the RAND Forces and Resources Policy Center, see http://www.rand.org/nsrd/ndri/centers/frp.html or contact the director (contact information is provided on the web page).

Contents

Figures and Tables

Figures

Tables

Summary

Background and Structure of the Spouse Education and Career Opportunities Program

In 2007, the U.S. Department of Defense (DoD)'s Military Community and Family Policy office established a portfolio of initiatives under the Spouse Education and Career Opportunities (SECO) program. These initiatives include career counseling services available through the SECO Call Center at Military OneSource; scholarships for testing, education, and training for portable career fields through the My Career Advancement Account Scholarship; avenues to connect spouses with potential employers through the Military Spouse Employment Partnership; and efforts by the DoD State Liaison Office to improve the portability of occupational licenses and credentials across state lines and to expand unemployment compensation eligibility to military spouses following their service member's permanent change of station moves.

SECO's purpose is to provide career development and employment assistance for military spouses. The key goals for SECO are reductions of the following among military spouses:

- unemployment (lack of employment among those wishing to work)
- underemployment (working fewer hours than desired or in jobs for which one is overqualified)
- employment gaps following moves
- wage gaps for military spouses relative to their counterparts who are married to civilians.

The ultimate aims of promoting spouse education and employment continuity are to improve satisfaction with military life, family financial stability, the health and wellness of the military community, retention of military personnel, and the overall readiness of the armed forces (Office of the Deputy Under Secretary of Defense, 2008).

The SECO program arose from growing evidence that military spouses tend to have more years of education than their civilian counterparts but are generally less likely to be employed and more likely to experience unemployment. Further, those who are employed tend to earn less, due in part to aspects of military life, such as frequent moves and depressed labor markets around military bases. This body of evidence has deepened presidential and congressional commitments to support a federal governmentwide approach to promoting military families; part of that approach includes evaluating whether federal education programs and efforts to support military spouse employment are cost-effective and working as intended.

Objectives of This Study

In early 2012, the Office of Cost Assessment and Program Evaluation in the Office of the Secretary of Defense required DoD's Military Community and Family Policy office to change the way it evaluated its SECO program, moving from assessment of processes to assessment of impact on users' lives. In December of that year, the U.S. Government Accountability Office (GAO) recommended that DoD describe its overall strategy for how programs should coordinate to help military spouse employment, and that it improve monitoring and evaluation of these programs.

This report provides RAND's proposed template for an internal monitoring system that Military Community and Family Policy can use to track how well the SECO program is being implemented and whether it is meeting short- and medium-term goals. The template's primary purpose is to equip staff with the ability to measure the performance of the program and gauge the extent to which it is producing intended outputs and meeting expected outcomes. While the internal monitoring system outlined in this report touches on how staff can document implementation of each initiative, it stops short of specifying how to conduct full evaluations of processes or outcomes.

The Value of an Internal Monitoring System

Internal monitoring can lead to stronger quality of services and program design. Program managers can undertake internal monitoring while a program or portfolio of programs is implemented, with the aim of improving design and functioning while in action. The process is designed to provide constant feedback on the progress of a program, the problems it is facing, and the efficiency with which it is being implemented. The ultimate purpose of an internal monitoring system is to enable program administrators to answer questions about functioning and monitor progress toward goals. In this case, internal monitoring is a dynamic process that requires an iterative cycle of assessment of collected data (typically, but not solely, quantitative data) to determine whether SECO initiatives are functioning as designed, providing optimum support to spouses, and if not, where efforts can be improved.

Internal monitoring differs from an *evaluation*, which is a rigorous and independent assessment of completed or ongoing activities. An evaluation can provide program managers with an objective assessment of the extent to which a program produced the intended outcomes and impacts and with an examination of the distribution of the benefits among different groups. Evaluations are also typically more rigorous than routine program monitoring in their procedures, design, and methodology, or they may involve deeper or more-extensive analysis (United Nations Evaluation Group, 2005). An internal monitoring system can be an effective and less costly way for an organization to: provide constant feedback on progress that programs are making in achieving their goals; identify potential problems at an early stage and propose possible midcourse corrections; monitor the accessibility of the program to all sectors of the target population; and monitor the efficiency with which the different components of a program are being implemented. This information can then be used to improve program design.

Proposed SECO Internal Monitoring System

RAND suggests five steps to develop and implement the SECO internal monitoring system:

Step 1. Describe the logic or theory of how activities are designed to meet the program's goals. As a first step in designing the monitoring and evaluation strategy for SECO, it is necessary to first identify the scope of the interventions, the specific effects SECO activities are designed to produce, and how they are thought to achieve them. This is undertaken by designing a *logic model*, which presents a snapshot of how the program is expected to work: a conceptual plan of program components, clear statements of measurable objectives or expected outcomes, the mechanisms by which objectives or outcomes will be met, and various external factors and participant characteristics that could influence outcomes but are outside the purview of program administrators.

Figure S.1 illustrates the logic model for SECO that RAND developed.

Step 2. Develop indicators. Once the logic model has been developed, it is critical to select key indicators that will be used to measure progress toward goals. RAND suggested that SECO select indicators that meet SMART criteria: **S**pecific, **M**easurable, **A**ctionable or **A**ppropriate, **R**eliable, and **T**ime-bound. RAND developed a suggested set of indicators for SECO program activities, outputs, short-term outcomes, and medium-term outcomes—noting which indicators were already collected by SECO, as well as those that were not and should be (see Appendix A). RAND analysis of SECO data sources found that Military Community and Family Policy collects information that describes activities and most inputs across the SECO program but that indicators for short- and medium-term outcomes are sparse. Indicators on short-term outcomes are available only for the My Career Advancement Account Scholarship and the Military Spouse

Figure S.1
RAND Logic Model of SECO Program

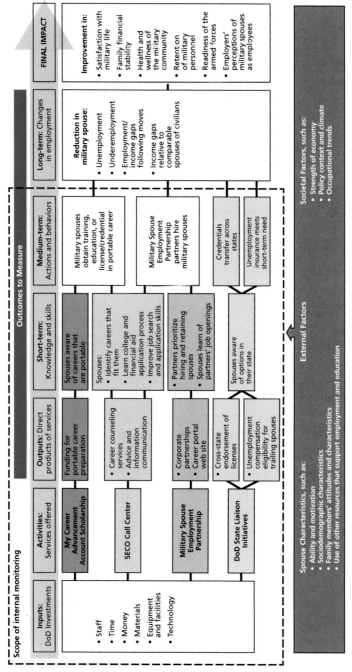

RAND *RR1013-S.1*

Employment Partnership, and indicators on medium-term outcomes are available only for the My Career Advancement Account Scholarship. In general, indicators for each component exist for the My Career Advancement Account Scholarship with multiple data sources available for all components (except short-term outcomes). Few indicators exist for the SECO Call Center. The DoD State Liaison Office only has one indicator for the activities component. If other initiatives are added to the SECO portfolio, Military Community and Family Policy can augment the indicator list.

Step 3. Identify benchmarks and targets. For managers to determine when or whether the SECO program is successful, the indicators developed in Step 2 for outputs and outcomes should have accompanying benchmarks and targets for performance. Progress can then be compared or measured relative to determined benchmarks or targets. Typically, targets are measurable finite goals and benchmarks are baselines or groups against which progress is compared. Without benchmarks or targets, it can be difficult to determine whether findings from analyses represent meaningful progress toward goals. RAND suggested that at specific milestone points (e.g., quarterly, annually), Military Community and Family Policy office staff could review the data collected on each indicator and compare progress with the benchmarks and targets developed in this step.

Step 4. Collect, organize, manage, and visualize the data collected into a Monitoring Matrix. Establishing a structure to process, organize, and visualize data over time is essential for creating an easy-to-use, pragmatic, and dependable monitoring system. Therefore, to maximize continuous tracking of each SECO initiative's performance, the next step is to organize data on the SMART indicators created in Step 2 alongside their accompanying targets and benchmarks created in Step 3 into what we call a *Monitoring Matrix*, commonly referred to in the civilian program evaluation field and in private-sector business as a *data dashboard* (see, for example, Marsh, Pane, and Hamilton, 2006; Ikemoto and Marsh, 2006; Swan, 2009; Ryan et al., 2014; Bors et al., 2015; Krapels et al., 2015). Data should be entered at specific time intervals and monitored on an ongoing basis. The Monitoring Matrix is not intended to be a static data collector; it is a tool that analyzes and visualizes data to support data-driven decisionmaking. This tool will allow Military Community and Family Policy staff to analyze data in various ways as deemed appropriate, including measuring indicators; identifying institutional arrangements and structures for gathering, analyzing, and reporting individual program data; and investing in developing staff skills and capacities to use the tool. The visualization of the data collected with the Monitoring Matrix will allow Military Community and Family Policy program staff to document trends and provide deeper understanding of what is occurring within programs. Example elements of the SECO Monitoring Matrix are provided in the report.

Step 5. Use data organized in the Monitoring Matrix to inform decisionmaking for ongoing improvements. By distilling the wide range of information organized in the Monitoring Matrix, Military Community and Family Policy staff can answer questions about program functioning and monitor progress toward program goals: tracking whether processes are operating as expected and whether activities are reaching expected outputs and short- or medium-term outcomes. They can also observe in a timely manner when unexpected trends emerge or whether a policy or program change that was made in response to shifts in the data may require further investigation. In addition to routinely monitoring the performance of the SECO program, Military Community and Family Policy can use the data to build capacity for a future implementation evaluation to determine whether the SECO program is "doing the work in the right way." Finally, Military Community and Family Policy can also use the information from the Monitoring Matrix and any evaluations its data support to manage the SECO program in a way that ensures its initiatives are "doing the right work," or achieving the desired outcomes and tracking the connections across activities' outputs, implementation, and attainment of desired outcomes (Knowlton and Phillips, 2013, p. 9).

Suggestions to Support Implementation of the SECO Internal Monitoring System

There are several challenges to implement and maintain the proposed SECO internal monitoring system. First, to measure progress on all components of the SECO logic model, additional indicators will need to be identified and collected through new or existing data sources. RAND analysis identified gaps in indicators that current data sources can provide. Appendix A lists the indicators that are available along with those that require additional or modified data collection efforts, which would greatly expand the indicators available to inform the monitoring system. For most of the additional indicators listed in Appendix A, additional data collection would come through two mechanisms: additional questions asked in the Active Duty Spouse Survey and a follow-up module added to the Customer Feedback Questionnaire administered to volunteer users of the MySECO portal for internal quality assurance purposes.

Second, staff will need to select appropriate benchmarks or targets to adequately measure the progress of each indicator, so staff can pinpoint the extent to which progress relative to benchmarks and targets is being made—or to determine why it is not. The development of benchmarks or targets should take into consideration any external factors that are delineated at the bottom of the SECO logic model depicted in Figure S.1. For example, if staff find that there is an uptick in spouse users of their offerings, they should examine what types of external factors (such as a downturn in the economy or a possible drawdown in troops) might be affecting spouse usage rates.

Third, staff's internal capacity to collect the data and analyze them, as well as an adequate technological infrastructure, will need to be put in place to ensure that the Monitoring Matrix is useful and provides the information necessary to support decisionmaking. A key to a useful and relevant internal monitoring system is to ensure that SECO program staff are aware of the need for the system; are included in discussions about the indicators, development of benchmarks or targets, and the design of the structure of the Monitoring Matrix; and that they are able to use the technology needed to employ and maintain it as a useful tool for analysis. Furthermore, SECO staff should communicate clearly with the contractors tasked with collecting data (e.g., My Career Advancement Account Scholarship data or Customer Feedback Questionnaire for internal quality assurance) so that data can be collected in a timely fashion and are reliable, valid, and error-free. Processes for data uploads to the Monitoring Matrix could be automated to ensure that data are collected and aggregated consistently across time.

Fourth, mileposts or reflection points will need to be built into staff schedules to guarantee use of the internal monitoring system to assess and manage the SECO program. For the SECO internal monitoring system to be useful, regular mileposts should indicate when Monitoring Matrix visualizations and analyses are reviewed and when decisions for assessing program performance or management can be made. Without regular reflection points, the internal monitoring system will lose its utility and could become a stagnant data collection effort, rather than an exercise to support decisionmaking to maximize the ongoing impact of the SECO program.

Acknowledgments

We would like to acknowledge the support and insights of our sponsors in the Office of the Deputy Assistant Secretary of Defense, Military Community and Family Policy: Dr. Cathy Flynn, Charles (Eddy) Mentzer, Lee McMahon, Yuko Whitestone, and former staff Aggie Byers and Meg O'Grady. They guided us on Military Community and Family Policy priorities for the SECO program and provided detailed information about each initiative. We also owe thanks to Pat Shanaghan at Military Community and Family Policy and Spencer Mann at BAM Technologies for reviewing with us in detail the types of content of the My Career Advancement Account Scholarship data fields. Marcus Beauregard helped us understand the Department of Defense State Liaison Office initiatives and limitations on the availability of state data that could help track their impact.

Our colleagues Amalia Miller and Andrew Morral provided input during an early stage of this project. We have also benefited from thoughtful feedback from Lisa Harrington, John Winkler, Paul Heaton, Jennifer Lewis, and Gretchen Jordan.

Abbreviations

ADSS	Active Duty Spouse Survey
DEERS	Defense Enrollment Eligibility Reporting System
DMDC	Defense Manpower Data Center
DoD	U.S. Department of Defense
DSLO	Department of Defense State Liaison Office
FY	fiscal year
GAO	U.S. Government Accountability Office
GPRAMA	Government Performance and Results Act Modernization Act of 2010
MyCAA	My Career Advancement Account
MSEP	Military Spouse Employment Partnership
OMB	United States Office of Management and Budget
PCS	permanent change of station
SECO	Spouse Education and Career Opportunities
SMART	Specific, Measurable, Actionable or Appropriate, Reliable, and Time-Bound

Monitoring the Military Spouse Education and Career Opportunities Program: Background and Study Objectives

Background

Research has found that military spouses tend to earn less than spouses of civilians and are less likely to be employed, even when they have more years of education or more work experience (Booth, 2003; Booth et al., 2000; Harrell et al., 2004; Heaton and Krull, 2012; Hisnanick and Little, 2014; Kniskern and Segal, 2010; Lim, Golinelli, and Cho, 2007). Features of military life—such as rigid and demanding work hours for military personnel, frequent permanent change of station (PCS) moves, and depressed labor markets around military bases—contribute to these differences in employment and earnings (Booth, 2003; Booth et al., 2000; Booth, Segal, and Bell, 2007; Castaneda and Harrell, 2008; Cooney, 2003; Cooney, De Angelis, and Segal, 2011; Cooke and Speirs, 2005; Harrell et al., 2004; Heaton and Krull, 2012; Hisnanick and Little, 2014; Little and Hisnanick, 2007; Kniskern and Segal, 2010; Lim, Golinelli, and Cho, 2007).

To mitigate the impact of the demands of military life, the U.S. Department of Defense (DoD) in 2007 established the Spouse Education and Career Opportunities (SECO) program, a portfolio of initiatives that provide career development and employment assistance for military spouses as a way to reduce unemployment, underemployment, and employment gaps following PCS moves, as well as to ameliorate wage gaps between military spouses and their counterparts who are married to civilians. The ultimate aims of SECO are to improve satisfaction with military life, family financial stability, health and wellness of the military community, retention of military personnel, and the overall readiness of the armed forces (Office of the Deputy Under Secretary of Defense, 2008).

DoD characterizes SECO as a part of its broader military family readiness system (DoD, 2012). The SECO program elements, described more fully in Chapter Two, include:

- career counseling services available through the SECO Call Center at Military OneSource
- resources for testing, education, and training for portable career fields, available through the My Career Advancement Account Scholarship
- avenues to connect spouses with potential employers through the Military Spouse Employment Partnership
- efforts by the DoD State Liaison Office to improve the portability of occupational licenses and credentials across state lines and to expand unemployment compensation eligibility to military spouses following their service member after a PCS move.

Calls for Program Monitoring and Evaluation

A clear priority for the federal government is to create and foster a culture of continuous improvement among federal agencies. The Government Performance and Results Act of 1993 (Public Law 103-62) and its successor, the Government Performance and Results Act Modernization Act (GPRAMA) of 2010 (Public Law 111-352) instituted a governmentwide requirement that federal agencies set goals and report annually on performance. Both laws guide federal agencies to establish strategic planning, performance planning, and performance reporting as a framework to track their programs' progress toward achieving agency missions. GPRAMA emphasizes the requirements of governmentwide and agency priority-setting and cross-organizational collaboration to achieve shared goals. The U.S. Office of Management and Budget's (OMB's) *Fiscal Year 2014 Analytic Perspectives for the Budget* (2013) operationalizes the GPRAMA 2010 for the federal government: It describes the federal performance framework, strategic and annual plans, the performance management cycle, the role of program evaluation, and detailed guidance on conducting program evaluations. This guidance requires federal leaders and managers to set specific short-term performance goals and indicators for their programs, as well as long-term goals and objectives, and lists six practices the White House has emphasized:

- goal-setting
- frequent measurement of performance and other indicators
- ongoing analysis
- use of evidence in decisionmaking
- data-driven reviews
- information dissemination that is timely, accessible, and user-friendly (OMB, 2013, p. 87).

Within this context, there have been multiple calls for an evaluation of the cost-effectiveness of federal efforts promoting military spouse employment and education, as well as an assessment of whether they meet the needs of the military spouses they were designed to help. In May 2010, President Barack Obama directed the National Security Staff to develop a coordinated, federal governmentwide approach to supporting military families. Subsequently, an interagency policy committee identified four priority areas to address the concerns and challenges of military families. The committee's report, *Strengthening our Military Families: Meeting America's Commitment* (White House, 2011), stated that one of the priorities was for a governmentwide commitment to develop career and educational opportunities for military spouses by:

- increasing opportunities for federal careers
- increasing opportunities for private-sector careers
- increasing access to educational advancement
- reducing barriers to employment and services due to different state policies and standards
- protecting the rights of service members and families (White House, 2011, p. 2).

The report concluded by asserting that, "each commitment has associated metrics and will undergo recurring assessments" (White House, 2011, p. 23).

In December 2010, U.S. Senator Tom Harkin, chairman of the Health, Education, Labor, and Pensions Committee, published a report (Harkin, 2010) questioning whether educational benefits for service members, veterans, and military spouses were benefiting for-profit schools more than they were benefiting the recipients. For-profit schools receive a significant share of military educational benefits, including funds provided for the education of military spouses. To inform the committee's inquiry, the Office of the Deputy Assistant Secretary of Defense for Military Community and Family Policy was called upon to provide statistics on data it was collecting on the My Career Advancement Account Scholarship, which was named explicitly in the report. Military Community and Family Policy decides which institutions it will approve as eligible to receive My Career Advancement Account Scholarships. It also documents whether schools are public or private and whether they are for-profit or nonprofit. During the first year of the My Career Advancement Account Scholarship, 46 percent of military spouse participants who were enrolled in degree-seeking programs were attending for-profit schools (about 41,869 spouses) (Harkin, 2010, p. 6). The report highlighted prior investigations demonstrating that the majority of students who enroll in for-profit schools accumulate debt but do not complete their course of study. Furthermore, it asserted that the default and low rate of loan repayment for those who do graduate calls into question whether those degrees lead to higher-paying jobs (Harkin, 2010, p. 17).[1] Thus, Harkin called upon Congress, DoD, and the Department of Veterans Affairs to investigate the quality and outcomes of education at for-profit schools to ensure that new federal military education benefits work as intended and that taxpayer dollars are spent wisely.

---

[1] Harkin states that "It is noteworthy that four of the five for-profit schools receiving the most Post-9/11 GI Bill funding in the first year have loan repayment rates of only 31 percent to 37 percent. The same four schools have at least one campus with a student loan default rate above 24 percent over three years" (p. 13).

In early 2012, the Office of Cost Assessment and Program Evaluation in the Office of the Secretary of Defense required that Military Community and Family Policy evaluate its military spouse programs, and emphasized that evaluations should focus on programs' impacts on users' lives rather than on program processes. In December 2012, the U.S. Government Accountability Office (GAO) recommended that DoD describe its overall strategy for how programs should coordinate to help military spouse employment and that DoD improve monitoring and evaluation of these programs.

Objectives of the Study

As a result of the increased emphasis on monitoring and evaluation in federal agencies, and specifically of programs that support military families, this report provides a template for an internal monitoring system that Military Community and Family Policy can use to document how the SECO program is being implemented and assess whether it is reaching short-term and medium-term goals in meeting the needs of spouses by supporting participants' awareness of opportunities and acquisition of skills and knowledge.

The primary purpose of this system is to equip staff with the ability to measure the performance of each initiative under SECO—to gauge the extent to which the SECO program is producing intended outputs and meeting expected outcomes. An internal monitoring system thereby could inform ongoing improvements to SECO programming. While the system outlined in this report touches on how staff can document implementation of each initiative, it stops short of elaborating on how staff can conduct a process evaluation to gauge how well processes are implemented.

The suggested internal monitoring system described in this report is part of a larger RAND study evaluating SECO program implementation and impact on military spouse education and employment. The other parts of the broader study include an analysis of 2012 Active Duty Spouse Survey (ADSS) responses from My Career Advancement Account Scholarship–eligible users and nonusers to learn more about the education and employment goals and barriers of these populations and to identify opportunities for SECO program improvement (Friedman, Miller, and Evans, 2015), and an evaluation study comparing My Career Advancement Account Scholarship users with nonusers. Additionally, a separate RAND analysis is under way to learn more about the progress the Military Spouse Employment Partnership has made in connecting employer partners with spouse users (Gonzalez et al., 2015). While there have been studies that explored employment or income of military spouses using single or repeated cross-sections of data (e.g., public-use Census samples, the Current Population Survey, military surveys), there has been no previous formal evaluation of the SECO program to assess implementation or to understand its potential effectiveness in improving the employability of spouses.

Military Community and Family Policy routinely has been gathering usage and performance statistics on each of its SECO initiatives. In fiscal year (FY) 2012, RAND developed a logic model (see Chapter Three) that articulates the overall strategy for the SECO program.[2] This logic model also served as a framework against which existing data sources could be identified and evaluated. RAND determined that although the My Career Advancement Account Scholarship was relatively new, it held the most potential of the SECO initiatives in terms of the ability to measure impact, as it had been collecting detailed individual-level data on participation. Furthermore, the 2012 ADSS included items that asked military spouses about their perspectives and use of My Career Advancement Account Scholarships, as well as about their education and employment preferences and experiences more broadly, thus providing the opportunity to gain additional insights for the My Career Advancement Account Scholarship initiative. Data on the SECO Call Center, the Military Spouse Employment Partnership, and DoD State Liaison Office activities and outcomes were insufficient for program evaluation. RAND also concluded that any attempts to conduct an assessment using only existing administrative datasets,

---

[2]   In a complementary effort, RAND also developed logic models to describe the features and intended outcomes of DoD, Department of Veterans Affairs, and Department of Education educational assistance programs available to military personnel to use while they are still in the service (Buryk et al., 2015).

such as military personnel databases or Social Security Administration earnings records, without also including SECO program data, could fail to capture impacts or misattribute differences in outcomes. That approach would be problematic because these administrative datasets contain too few SECO outcomes and too little information on potentially confounding variables.

Against this backdrop of other efforts, Military and Community Family Policy has undertaken to document and understand the performance of SECO. A core priority of this project was to assist in continuing efforts to develop metrics that could be mapped to the logic model.

In the remainder of this chapter, we explain how internal monitoring and evaluation complement each other. We then provide a road map for the remainder of the report.

The Value of an Internal Monitoring System

Program designers, managers, and key stakeholders typically want to know whether programs are being implemented properly and whether they are meeting their intended goals. Answering these questions requires *program evaluation*,[3] a rigorous and independent assessment

---

[3] A high-quality, comprehensive program evaluation includes process, outcome, and impact evaluations. *Process evaluations* (also known as implementation assessments) ask, "Are systems in place?" They document and analyze whether and how well services are delivered as intended (GAO, 2011; Wholey, Hatry, and Newcomer, 2010; Rossi, Lipsey, and Freeman, 2004). This kind of evaluation assesses how targeted participants experience the program, explains variations in program delivery, and describes how a program is organized (Patton, 2008). It identifies program strengths and areas needing improvement, and it documents whether initiatives are functioning to promote the programs' success (GAO, 2011; Wholey, Hatry, and Newcomer, 2010; Rossi, Lipsey, and Freeman, 2004). *Outcome evaluations* ask, "Are we making progress in achieving our goals?" They can help stakeholders assess program performance in terms of progress and meeting goals. Outcome evaluations assess the outputs and outcomes (including unintended effects) to judge program effectiveness and can assess how outcomes are produced (GAO, 2011). An analysis of program effectiveness, when coupled with a process evaluation, can reveal ways to improve effectiveness (Rossi, Lipsey, and Freeman, 2004). *Impact evaluations* ask, "What kind of broad social change has the program made in the community?" They differ from outcome evaluations in that they focus on longer-term changes. Furthermore, outcome evaluations typically focus on individuals targeted by the program (e.g., spouses) rather than the community as a whole. Impact evalu-

of either completed or ongoing activities to provide evidence about program effectiveness. Program evaluations have been recommended for federal programs so that decisionmakers have the information they need to judge programs' progress, efficiency, and effectiveness (GAO, 2011; OMB, 2013, p. 91).

Key to an evaluation is *performance measurement*, or "ongoing monitoring and reporting of program accomplishments, particularly progress toward pre-established goals" (GAO, 2011, p. 2). Program staff or managers can participate in performance measurement and data tracking, while a program is implemented, with the aim of improving the program's design and functioning while in action (United Nations Evaluation Group, 2005; GAO, 2011; OMB, 2013). It is this type of monitoring, or performance measurement, that is the primary focus of this report.

Evaluations and internal monitoring are both systematic processes for understanding what a program, initiative, or reform does and how well it is doing it. Their aims are similar: to provide information that can help inform decisions, improve performance, and achieve planned results. However, the key distinction is that internal monitoring is designed to provide constant and continual feedback on the progress of a program, the problems it is facing, and the efficiency with which it is being implemented (Bamberger and Hewitt, 1986, p. 1), typically conducted by program staff. In contrast, evaluations are done independently, typically by an external body, to provide program managers with an objective assessment of the extent to which a program produced the intended outcomes and impacts and to examine the distribution of benefits among different groups (Bamberger and Hewitt, 1986; GAO, 2011, p. 2). Evaluations are also typically more rigorous in their procedures, design, or methodology, or they may involve deeper or more-extensive analysis than internal monitoring (United Nations Evaluation Group, 2005).

Evaluation and internal monitoring are complementary tools for providing credible information, well-grounded decisionmaking,

---

ations can also assess the "net effect" of a program by comparing outcomes with estimates of what would have happened in the absence of the program.

and transparency. Well-planned and well-conducted evaluations and internal monitoring are an integral part of an ongoing cycle of program planning and development, implementation, and improvement (Patton, 2008). Internal monitoring complements evaluation and provides a reliable flow of information during implementation. Information analyzed through internal monitoring can therefore be used to

- ensure that the program service is executed according to plan and is reaching all sectors of the population it is intended to serve
- identify potential problems at an early stage and propose possible solutions or improvements to support midcourse corrections
- provide constant feedback on progress that programs are making in achieving their goals that will be useful in the design and implementation of subsequent services (World Bank Operations Evaluation Department, 1996; World Bank, 1994).

A synthesis of previous research (Baumberger and Hewitt, 1986; Haims et al. 2011, McDavis and Hawthorne, 2006) indicates that a strong internal monitoring system includes four key components:

1. clear statements of measurable objectives or outcomes and the mechanisms by which a program is designed to meet those objectives or outcomes
2. a structured set of indicators, covering outputs of goods and services generated by the program and the intended impact on program participants (these indicators should include targets and benchmarks against which progress can be compared or measured)
3. a process for collecting data and managing records so that the data required for measuring indicators are compatible with existing statistics, and are available at reasonable cost (this includes institutional arrangements and structures for gathering, analyzing, and reporting individual program data, and for investing in capacity building)

4. processes for using findings from monitoring efforts to inform decisionmaking and continuous improvements.

The information collected in an internal monitoring system also can support a more formal evaluation. Aggregating and analyzing data collected via internal monitoring, but using more-sophisticated methods through an evaluation, can reveal trends and impact or lack of impact on target populations. Thus, to provide a foundation for larger-scale program evaluation, it is important that program data are not used solely by program vendors and/or managers, but are also stored so they can be made available to evaluators. Additionally, these data must be archived, as the size and time frame must be sufficient to permit identification of trends and effects.

Organization of the Report

In the remainder of this report, we outline a proposed detailed internal monitoring system to support informed decisionmaking that would enhance and build upon the SECO monitoring efforts that Military Community and Family Policy has already been developing. Chapter Two describes the core SECO program at the time of this report. Chapter Three outlines the key components of the proposed internal monitoring system, which follow the four components of a strong internal monitoring system, dividing them into five concrete steps with example indicators that Military Community and Family Policy can collect to inform its decisionmaking. Chapter Four concludes with recommendations of ways for Military Community and Family Policy to continue monitoring the SECO program. Appendix A provides a list of indicators that can be used to track progress of the SECO program, as well as associated data sources from which the indicators can be drawn. Appendix B documents additional questions that RAND suggests be asked of respondents immediately upon completion of the MySECO Portal Customer Feedback Questionnaire and three to six months later; Military Community and Family Policy can use the responses to gauge immediate changes in spouse respondents' short- and medium-term outcomes.

CHAPTER TWO

Overview of the SECO Program

Introduction

As noted at the beginning of Chapter One, DoD's SECO program includes the My Career Advancement Account Scholarship, career counseling services available through the SECO Call Center at Military OneSource, the Military Spouse Employment Partnership, and DoD State Liaison Office initiatives to expand unemployment compensation eligibility for trailing military spouses and to secure cross-state endorsements of professional certifications and licenses.

While other DoD initiatives designed to promote the education and employment of military spouses exist, they are outside the scope of the project because they are not part of SECO. For example, DoD's Military Spouse Preference program, established under the Military Family Act of 1985, provides hiring mechanisms through which military spouses can be matched with certain types of DoD civilian jobs and/or positions covered by non–congressionally appropriated funding, although spouses do not need to go through this program to obtain DoD jobs (GAO, 2012). From FY 2002 through FY 2011, about 12,500 military spouses were hired as DoD civilians through this program (GAO, 2012, p. 22). DoD data on the use of the Military Spouse Preference program to obtain nonappropriated-funded positions are inconsistent, but in June 2012, about 26,000 spouses held positions in these typically high-turnover service jobs, which include positions in military installation stores, child care centers, and recreation programs (GAO, 2012, pp. 20, 22). Other DoD efforts that support spouses' abilities to pursue education and employment opportunities include employment services, child care centers, and youth programs at military installations, but these are also outside the scope of this study despite having the same overarching goals as the SECO program that is under consideration.

Within the Office of the Under Secretary for Personnel and Readiness, the Office of the Deputy Assistant Secretary of Defense for Military Community and Family Policy is responsible for quality-of-life policies and programs to support service members and their families. The key Military Community and Family Policy office goals for the SECO program are a reduction in the following among military spouses:

- unemployment (lack of employment among those wishing to work)
- underemployment (working fewer hours than desired or in jobs for which one is overqualified)
- employment gaps following moves
- wage gaps for military spouses relative to their counterparts who are married to civilians.

The ultimate aims of promoting spouse education and employment continuity are to improve satisfaction with military life, family financial stability, the health and wellness of the military community, retention of military personnel, and the overall readiness of the armed forces (Office of the Deputy Under Secretary of Defense, 2008).

The remainder of this chapter reviews the primary efforts under way as of July 2015. Where citations are not provided, information comes from Military Community and Family Policy information sheets, briefings, or direct communication with Military Community and Family Policy.

The My Career Advancement Account Scholarship

The DoD My Career Advancement Account Scholarship[1] provides up to $4,000 in tuition and examination assistance for eligible spouses

---

[1]   Much of this section describing the My Career Advancement Account Scholarship was also published in another report produced by this research project (Friedman, Miller, and Evans, 2015).

pursuing associate's degrees, occupational certificates, or licenses in portable career fields. DoD defines portable careers as high-demand, high-growth careers identified by the Department of Labor as likely to be sustainable over time and to have job openings near military duty locations. The My Career Advancement Account Scholarship emphasizes these careers based on the following rationale:

> (Attainment of) a portable degree or credential funded with a CAA [Career Advancement Account] will help military spouses enter and advance in the workforce even as they relocate when their service member spouses transfer to other bases. A longer-term goal . . . is to encourage the retention of the service member in the military by improving his or her spouse's job prospects and increasing the satisfaction of the entire family with life in the military. (Zaveri, Pisciotta, and Rosenberg, 2009, p. 1)

The My Career Advancement Account Scholarship is relatively new and has gone through three iterations. Across these iterations, its consistent goal has been to support spouses in their pursuit of careers that are better able to weather the frequent moves of the military lifestyle.

The first version of the My Career Advancement Account Scholarship began in July 2007, when DoD and the Department of Labor collaborated to launch the Military Spouse Career Advancement Account Demonstration on a small scale at 18 installations in eight states.[2] The goal of the initiative was to employ military spouses in portable careers to help manage the "mobile military lifestyle" (Office of the Deputy Under Secretary of Defense, 2008, p. 1). To be eligible, military spouses had to have a high school diploma or General Education Development certificate at the time of application and be married to a service member with at least one year remaining at his or her current duty station. Eligible spouses at the participating installations were provided with up to $3,000 a year for two years to use toward tuition, fees, or other relevant expenses at accredited two-year colleges and technical training centers or toward fees required for career

---

[2] The states were California, Colorado, Florida, Georgia, Hawaii, Maine, North Carolina, and Washington.

credentials and licenses. As of May 2009, about 17 months after the selected states were to begin providing these awards, 5,366 grants were awarded (Needels and Zaveri, 2009, p. 17). An implementation study documented successes and challenges of that initial effort, and found in group discussions that spouses participated to

- further career and job prospects
- improve themselves and their self-esteem
- further their education
- contribute to family financial well-being
- engage in a positive distraction during their service member's deployment (Zaveri, Pisciotta, and Rosenberg, 2009, p. 57).

The evaluation of the demonstration effort was conducted too early to be able to assess individual-level short- and long-term outcomes: Most spouses had not completed their training or employment at that time (Needels and Zaveri, 2009; Zaveri, Pisciotta, and Rosenberg, 2009).

Following that demonstration, a full-scale My Career Advancement Account Scholarship tuition assistance initiative was launched across DoD in 2009 to promote employment and portable career opportunities by offering up to $6,000 a year to any military spouses. In less than a year, DoD was overwhelmed by the demand: 136,000 spouses enrolled, for an estimated $250 million in benefits (Harkin, 2010, p. 6). The budget would not sustain an initiative of this scale, and the My Career Advancement Account Scholarship was closed to any new applicants. To save the scholarship and contain costs, DoD scaled it back in 2010 by limiting eligibility, approved uses, and the amount of the scholarships (Harkin, 2010, p. 6).

To further support spouses' abilities to move realistically and efficiently toward their education and occupational goals, SECO has required since 2012 that spouses who apply for a My Career Advancement Account Scholarship consult with the career counselors at the SECO Call Center. As we will describe in greater detail later in this chapter, those career counselors can help military spouses make decisions about which careers to pursue, develop an educational plan, and access additional scholarship information, should the spouse need funds beyond those available. My Career Advancement Account Scholarship recipients also must register for the Military Spouse Employment Partnership, which is designed to help them locate job opportunities. The remainder of this section describes the eligibility, approved uses, amount of awards, and usage of the My Career Advancement Account Scholarship, as of publication of this report.

Eligibility Requirements

The strategy for the redesigned My Career Advancement Account Scholarship is to focus on the spouse population most likely to have the greatest need for assistance and on courses of study likely to provide the most direct and immediate benefits to military spouses' employment opportunities. In October 2010, DoD launched a redesigned My Career Advancement Account Scholarship that restricted eligibility to spouses of military personnel in the earliest career ranks and pay grades.[3] Eligible spouses cannot be on active duty, and must be married to service members who are serving on active-duty Title 10 orders and in the pay grades of E-1 to E-5, W-1 to W-2, and O-1 to O-2. These military personnel tend to be in their first term of service, so there is also the possibility that the scholarship could serve as a retention tool. Educational benefits from the Post-9/11 GI Bill cannot be transferred to spouses until military personnel have at least six years of service in the armed forces, so most of these spouses would not yet be able to acquire funds from that source. Spouses who do not take advantage of this benefit before their spouses are promoted out of these pay grades lose the opportunity to do so.

Approved Uses

The My Career Advancement Account Scholarships pay for education, training, and testing in portable careers only, which covers hundreds of occupations falling into a diverse range of career fields. The original demonstration project of the My Career Advancement Account Scholarship specified five career fields that met this focus: construction, education, financial services, health care, and information technology. In response to feedback from military spouses, the My Career Advance-

---

[3] Most warrant officers are well advanced in their military careers, but for some Army aviators, this is the entry-level pay grade.

ment Account Scholarship expanded the career fields to include human resources, hospitality, homeland security, and business administration (Needels and Zaveri, 2009, p. 24). A complete list of portable career fields and a sample of approved occupations are listed in Table 2.1.

Scholarship funds can be used for tuition assistance for associate's degrees, occupational licenses, and certificates in portable careers. The scholarship supports pursuit of a high school equivalency certificate or diploma only as a part of a plan to obtain one of these degrees, licenses, or certificates, not as an end in and of itself. The scholarship does not support general studies or the pursuit of bachelor's or graduate degrees. Tuition for graduate-level courses that are part of an approved educational plan or for necessary continuing education in an approved career field also may be authorized.

In addition to tuition, scholarships can cover the costs associated with recertification, occupational license, or credential examinations. This can include courses at any level (including at the bachelor's and graduate levels) that are required as part of the recertification, license,

Table 2.1
Sample Portable Occupations by Career Field

Career Field	Sample Occupations
Aerospace	Aircraft mechanic, aircraft service technician
Animal services	Animal groomer, animal trainer, veterinarian
Automotive services and transportation	Automotive mechanic, police/fire/ambulance dispatcher
Business, finance, and administration	Accountant, real estate agent, tax preparer
Construction	Carpenter, interior designer, painter, welder
Education	Child care worker, K–12 teacher, librarian
Energy	Electrical power-line installer and repairer
Health and human services	Dentist, dietician, medical billing, psychologist
Homeland security	Detective, firefighter, police officer, security guard
Hospitality	Bartender, chef, lifeguard, event planner
Information technology	Database administrator, software engineer
Legal	Court reporter, lawyer, paralegal
Skilled trades	Barber, journalist, nail technician, translator/interpreter

SOURCE: SECO, 2016.

or credential examination. For example, a teacher holding a bachelor's degree who needs professional recertification in a new state following a PCS move can use funds from a scholarship to pay for any courses or exams required for that recertification. Many occupations and professions are regulated by state licenses and certificates: A few examples not included in Table 2.1 include truck driver, cosmetologist, electrician, licensed practical nurse, physical therapist, home inspector, computer network administrator, pharmacy technician, and human resource specialist.

Scholarship Amounts

Since October 2010, scholarships have provided a maximum education benefit of $4,000, with an annual fiscal year cap of $2,000. Annual cap waivers are available for licensure and certificate programs if there is an upfront tuition cost that exceeds $2,000 (up to the maximum education benefit of $4,000). This scholarship is not taxable. The funds are sent one school term at a time, directly to the training or license/certification testing institution, not to spouses. Military Community and Family Policy must approve the accredited institution or testing facility before granting the scholarship. Spouses must be able to finish their program of study within three years from the start date of the first sponsored course: Funds are no longer available after that expiration date. Spouses will also lose access to funds if they become ineligible during this period (e.g., through divorce, by becoming active-duty themselves, or if their service member is promoted out of the eligible pay grade or leaves the military).

Use of the My Career Advancement Account Scholarship Since October 2010

SECO accepts all eligible spouses who apply for a scholarship for an approved course of study at an approved institution (i.e., there is no set number of scholarships for which spouses must compete). DoD reports that 101,144 spouses received the My Career Advancement Account Scholarship funds between the redesign at the end of October 2010 and the end of December 2014.

Table 2.2 shows the estimated number of associate's degrees, certificates, and licenses obtained by military spouses using the My Career Advancement Account Scholarship in that three-year time frame.

Table 2.2
My Career Advancement Account Scholarship Education Plans Estimated Completed Between October 25, 2010 and December 31, 2014

Education Plan	Estimated Number Completed
Associate's degree	8,075
Occupational certificate/credential	26,621
Occupational license	1,511
Total	**36,207**

SOURCE: Data for the My Career Advancement Account Scholarship provided by the Office of the Deputy Assistant Secretary of Defense for Military Community and Family Policy.

These numbers are estimates because schools did not always directly confirm completion of the educational plan. In some cases, however, the school indicated that the final course or the occupational license or certification exam was successfully completed with a passing grade. These numbers likely underestimate completion, as spouses who lost eligibility while still in school would have no incentive to return to the system and record that they completed the education plan.

The SECO Call Center

The Military OneSource SECO Call Center (formerly the Military Spouse Career Center) offers online and telephone services to assist active-duty, guard, and reserve spouses with any type of education or career goal, including the pursuit of graduate degrees or general studies. The SECO Call Center provides free career counseling services to all military spouses, regardless of the component or pay grade of their service member. In the first quarter of 2015, the call center fielded 28,641 calls. Of those, 26,937 were from spouses connected with the My Career Advancement Account Scholarship, the remaining 1,704 were from other spouses.

The SECO Call Center requires that its counselors hold education and credential requirements appropriate for advising military spouses on how to establish and achieve education and career goals. Two types of counselors staff the center: SECO Advisors and SECO Counselors.

SECO Advisors are the point of entry into the SECO Call Center. An advisor takes a call and determines what level of support the spouse needs. If it is a straightforward information-and-referral call (for example, "how do I know if my school participates in the My Career Advancement Account?") then the advisor will respond accordingly. If the spouse is in need of a more personalized service (e.g., reviewing a resume, developing an individual career plan, or strategizing a job search), then the advisor will refer the caller to a specialty consultation with a SECO Counselor. Advisors must possess, at a minimum, a bachelor's degree with at least four years of experience in education, career, or employment counseling. A preferred qualification includes a National Certified Counselor credential issued by the National Commission for Certifying Agencies or a current credential issued by the National Association for Workforce Development Professionals or the National Board of Certified Counselors.

SECO Counselor positions require a higher level of qualifications than advisors, given that they will be providing one-on-one consultative support. They must possess, at a minimum, a master's degree with at least four years of experience in education, career, or employment counseling. They must hold a current credential issued by the National Association for Workforce Development Professionals or the National Board of Certified Counselors or hold the National Certified Counselor credential from the National Commission for Certifying Agencies.

In addition to call center support, extensive advice and career-relevant information is available online through the SECO Call Center website, including information about SECO and other DoD programs. Communication forms include blog postings, e-magazines, self-help articles, documents that can be downloaded, webinars, and links to other websites. The SECO website's information is organized according to four pillars: career exploration; education, training, and licensing; employment readiness; and career connections.

Career Exploration

Through the call center, military spouses can speak with a SECO Counselor. These experts help spouses identify careers that match their interests, preferences, strengths, and other factors. The career counselors can provide spouses with information about job markets, employment trends, and earning potential metrics and educate them about a range of work options, such as telecommuting, job sharing, and starting a business. This service also aims to educate spouses about their potential eligibility for hiring priorities, such as DoD's Military Spouse Preference program described at the beginning of this chapter.

Education, Training, and Licensing
The intent of the SECO Call Center is also to help spouses create a personal plan to secure the career preparation they need. They can call in to obtain guidance on selecting a school and to learn about their financial aid options, including federal grants, student loans, My Career Advancement Account Scholarship funds and the Post-9/11 Education Benefits Transfer, whereby service members can transfer their military educational benefits to family members. The center is also designed to help spouses learn about state licensure initiatives that may permit them to work in a new home state under their previous license while working toward the new requirements.

Employment Readiness
Employment readiness services include advice from both SECO counselors and local installation employment specialists expected to be familiar with resources and opportunities in a given installation's community. These services focus on assisting spouses with resume-writing and interviewing skills, job search techniques, and preparations for relocations. These services are also intended to provide spouses with assistance in finding child care and learning about transportation options, such as public transportation and ride-sharing programs.

Career Connections
Military spouses may benefit not only from help identifying and preparing for good jobs but also from help finding those jobs. Under the career connections pillar, the SECO Call Center aims to make sure spouses are aware that many private and government employers are interested in hiring military spouses and that they should identify themselves as such when they apply. Spouses are directed to the Mili-

tary Spouse Employment Partnership web portal, as well as other job posting sites, such as USAJobs.gov and CareerOneStop.com.

The Military Spouse Employment Partnership

DoD is actively seeking to improve employment opportunities for military spouses through partnerships with employers. The Military Spouse Employment Partnership,[4] launched on June 29, 2011, is built upon the Army Employment Partnership, which had already recruited 52 employer partners since its inception in 2003. DoD refers to its Military Spouse Employment Partnership partners as "corporate partners," although not all are corporations. As of July 2015, the Military Spouse Employment Partnership had grown to 282 partners and included small or regional businesses, global businesses, defense contractors, universities, federal agencies, and nongovernmental organizations. Examples illustrate the diversity of the partners as well as their sheer potential for employing spouses: 24 Hour Fitness, 3M, Geico, MetLife, Safeway, American Red Cross, Home Depot, Hyatt, General Dynamics, INOVA, Microsoft, Starbucks, Toys "R" Us, CVS Health, Amazon.com, Verizon, Navy Exchange, Hitachi, Walmart, Goodwill Industries, Tutor.com, Armed Forces Bank, H & R Block, American Bar Association, and the Social Security Administration.[5] The Military Spouse Employment Partnership includes the Military Spouse Ambassador Network, which is designed to leverage the social networking skills of nonprofit organizations that support military spouses by enlisting them in spreading the word about available benefits and services of SECO and the importance of portable career choices for spouses of career military personnel.

Military Spouse Employment Partnership partners sign a statement of support with the armed forces that they will

---

[4] This initiative is not to be confused with the Military Spouse Preference hiring program, described at the beginning of this chapter.

[5] A complete list of partners is available at the Military Spouse Employment Partnership Career Portal (undated-b).

fulfill their commitment to support military spouses by agreeing to:

- identify and promote portable and sustainable career employment opportunities
- post job openings and provide a link to the corporate human resources employment page on the Military Spouse Employment Partnership Career Portal
- mentor new Military Spouse Employment Partnership partners
- Participate in the following Military Spouse Employment Partnership events:
  - New Partner Orientation
  - Annual Partner Meeting
  - New Partner Signing and Induction Ceremony. (Military Spouse Employment Partnership, 2014)

Military Spouse Employment Partnership partner activities may also include participating in job fairs, mentoring spouse employees, and building relations with military installation family support center staff who help spouses find jobs. Military spouses can register through the Military Spouse Employment Partnership Career Portal website (undated-a) to search and apply for job openings with Military Spouse Employment Partnership companies. Through this offering, the partnership aims to help military spouses find job openings with employers committed to hiring military spouses and to facilitating job transfers for them after moves. The ability of spouses to transfer jobs within the same organization can prevent a loss of seniority or a break in employment that might otherwise follow a change in location.[6]

The Department of Defense State Liaison Office Initiatives

The DoD State Liaison Office was created in 2004 to work with states to address military family issues. Among its activities are two efforts

---

[6] More information about the Military Spouse Employment Partnership is available in Gonzalez et al. (2015).

directly related to spouse income and employment: expansion of unemployment compensation and out-of-state credentialing.

Expansion of Unemployment Compensation Eligibility for Military Spouses Following a Move

For most active-duty military personnel, frequent moves are a part of life. These moves can disrupt the employment of military spouses, who may not be able to find employment right away at their new location. Although reassignment and relocation are requirements in the military, many states treat spouses who leave their jobs to move with their service member the same as other people who quit their jobs. This means these military spouses are ineligible for unemployment compensation available to those who are fired or laid off, a benefit that could help bridge the employment gap following a mandatory military move.

To address this limitation, the DoD State Liaison Office has been working with state lawmakers since 2004 to expand unemployment compensation eligibility for military spouses following a move. This benefit has gradually grown over time, as more and more legislatures have adopted this option. DoD is tracking the number of states covering trailing military spouses and the percentage of spouses covered (as spouses are not equally distributed across all states). According to Military Community and Family Policy, 39 states and the District of Columbia as of FY 2011 had extended unemployment compensation eligibility to trailing spouses, which covered 85 percent of military spouses.[7] When we reviewed the status in March 2013, only six states had not signed on: Idaho, Louisiana, North Dakota, Ohio, Vermont, and Virginia. Virginia was key because, according to initiative representatives, it is host to approximately 11 percent of active-duty military spouses in the nation. By May 2015, Virginia and Vermont had joined. Thus, at the time this study was conducted, only four states had still not passed supportive legislation, and the DoD State Liaison Office estimates that about 97 percent of the spouse population residing in the United States are now covered.

---

[7] Some states cover any spouse, whether a military spouse or not, moving to accompany their husband or wife to a new job in a new state.

The funding for unemployment insurance for spouses comes from a premium paid by private-sector employers. The amount is based on the number of workers, salary (up to a cap), and the "experience rating" of the employer, which is a measure of how many of the employer's workers have collected unemployment insurance benefits in the past. One potential challenge to allowing military spouses to collect unemployment insurance following a move is that employers that hire spouses potentially bear a greater cost burden (in terms of premium payments) because the employer's experience rating could subsequently rise with each military spouse that collects unemployment insurance. To prevent this circumstance from leading to discrimination against military spouses, the DoD State Liaison Office notes that many states stipulate that unemployment compensation claims associated with these military spouses do not accrue to employers' unemployment filing experience rating (Military OneSource, undated).

The DoD State Liaison Office chief confirms that staff do not have visibility on the impact of this SECO initiative. The DoD State Liaison Office does not have state, survey, or any other data that would allow it to know how many spouses have received this benefit or how many dollars have been spent to support unemployed military spouses following a move. The states have no incentive to track this information, so obtaining it is not a simple issue of access but one of collection. The DoD State Liaison Office also has no information about the level of awareness of this benefit among military spouses: when or how the change might have been publicized and whom that publicity might have reached. The DoD State Liaison Office does have records documenting the date the new legislation passed in each of the states that have adopted it, although the legislation does not necessarily take effect on those dates.

Agreements Across States Regarding Out-of-State Credentials for Military Spouses Following a Move

Using data from the Annual Social and Economic supplement of the Current Population Survey, a 2012 Department of the Treasury and DoD report estimated that nearly 35 percent of military spouses in the labor force need occupational licenses or certification in their fields and that military spouses are ten times more likely than their civilian counterparts to move across state lines (U.S. Department of Treasury and Department of Defense, 2012, p. 3). These estimates are similar to those from the 2012 ADSS, where 33 percent of spouses reported that their occupation requires a certification, and 27 percent reported that it requires a state-issued license (Defense Manpower Data Center [DMDC], 2013, p. 104). Occupations requiring state licenses that are common among military spouses include teaching, registered nursing, and accounting and auditing; common occupations requiring state certifications include child care, nursing/psychiatric/home health aide work, and dental assistant work (U.S. Department of Treasury and Department of Defense, 2012, p. 10). These are also many of the occupations considered portable and eligible for the My Career Advancement Account scholarships.

The DoD State Liaison Office has also worked with state governments to make it easier for military spouses with state licenses or certificates to work in their career fields following a military relocation. As with unemployment insurance, this benefit has grown gradually, as an increasing number of states offer some sort of accommodation to ease the transition for spouses in these types of occupations. As of March 2013, 28 states provided some provisions in this regard, either through passing legislation, existing statutes that already supported portability, or signing an executive order supporting license portability. By June 2016, New York was the only state remaining that had not made at least some changes in this direction, although a bill to do so was active in the state legislature.

Three types of desired state actions are described by the DoD State Liaison Office as:

- **Obtainable Endorsement:** Modify license by endorsement to allow options that accommodate gaps in employment for military spouses with active licenses from another state.
- **Temporary License:** Provide temporary licenses to allow a military spouse with a current license to secure employment while completing state requirements or while awaiting verification for an endorsement.
- **Expedited License:** Expedite procedures for regulatory department or board approval to provide opportunity

for spouses to obtain an endorsed or temporary license. (USA4MilitaryFamilies, 2016)

Military spouses in occupations requiring licenses or certifications stand to gain a great deal by not having their options limited to giving up their chosen career, not moving along with their service member, or suffering employment gaps and repeating licensure/certification processes every time they move. However, the actual provisions adopted vary by state: As of June 2016, 35 states allow endorsement of military spouses' active credentials from another state; 43 permit temporary licenses, and 34 offer expedited license procedures (USA4MilitaryFamilies, 2016). Furthermore, the vast majority of the states cover occupations in health-related fields and commercial occupations but not professional occupations, such as teaching or practicing law.

As with the unemployment insurance initiative, our point of contact at the DoD State Liaison Office confirms that staff there do not have visibility into the impact of these initiatives. There are no data collected on how many spouses have benefited from the different types of provisions described (obtainable endorsement, temporary license, expedited license) since each state adopted its agreement. The effort that would be required for the states to try to track the usage rates by military spouse across all of the occupational fields makes doing so infeasible. Here too, the DoD State Liaison Office has no information about the level of awareness of this benefit among military spouses.

Conclusion

DoD has invested and continues to invest significant resources in the SECO program elements, each of which takes a different approach toward reducing military spouse unemployment, underemployment, employment gaps following moves, and wage gaps relative to civilian spouses. In the next chapter, we describe the internal monitoring system SECO could use to document and assess the implementation of initiatives and their progress toward these goals.

CHAPTER THREE

Proposed SECO Internal Monitoring System

This chapter applies the four components of a strong internal monitoring system introduced in Chapter One to support Military Community and Family Policy's SECO program. To recap, these are:

1. clear statements of measurable objectives or outcomes and the mechanisms by which an initiative is designed to meet those objectives or outcomes
2. a structured set of indicators with accompanying targets and benchmarks, against which progress can be compared or measured
3. a process for collecting data and managing records
4. processes for using findings from monitoring efforts to inform decisionmaking and continuous improvements.

As the Military Community and Family Policy office develops its SECO internal monitoring system, RAND has suggested that the office build upon existing data collection and analysis efforts it already has under way and split the second component (develop indicators with accompanying benchmarks or targets) into two separate steps, creating a five-step process:

1. Describe the logic or theory of how activities are designed to meet the SECO program's goals. This will provide a conceptual plan of the program, clear statements of potentially measurable objectives or outcomes, and the mechanisms by which each SECO activity is designed to meet those objectives or outcomes.

2. Specify structured indicators to measure the goals and objectives outlined in the logic model.
3. Determine targets and benchmarks for the set of indicators, against which progress can be compared or measured.
4. Collect, organize, and manage data in a Monitoring Matrix, so that the data required for measuring indicators are compatible with existing statistics and are available at reasonable cost. This includes institutional arrangements and structures for gathering, analyzing, and reporting individual initiative data and for investing in staff's capacity to collect and utilize the data.
5. Analyze the data organized into the Monitoring Matrix to inform decisionmaking and continuous improvements or make midcourse corrections. This information should inform the cycle of continuous improvement and act as a feedback mechanism to allow Military Community and Family Policy to answer:
    a. What happened in the past period?
        ◦ Were processes implemented as designed?
        ◦ Are expected outputs occurring?
        ◦ Are short- and medium-term outcomes being met?
        ◦ How does progress compare to benchmarks or targets?
    b. If goals were not met, is further study or inquiry required to determine why?
        ◦ Are there external factors that need to be considered?
        ◦ Do other partners need to be included to improve meeting goals?
        ◦ Do benchmarks or targets need adjustment?

These steps are illustrated in Figure 3.1 and described in detail in the remainder of this chapter.

Step 1. Describe the Logic of the SECO Program

The first step in a SECO internal monitoring system is to identify the scope of the SECO initiatives, the specific effects they are designed to produce, and how they are thought to achieve them. This strategy is

Figure 3.1
Five Steps for Developing the SECO Internal Monitoring System

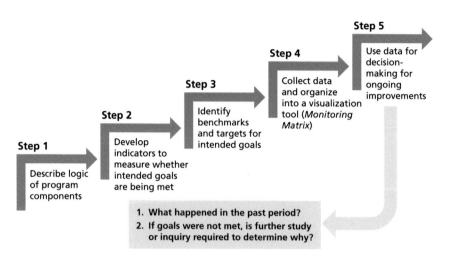

RAND RR1013-3.1

often achieved through the design of a *logic model*. Program evaluators have often discovered disagreement within organizations about what resources or activities are within the scope of a program, what specific outcomes those activities are designed to achieve, and through which mechanisms the programs could achieve those outcomes (Wholey et al., 2010). Logic models (also referred to as *theories of action* or *theories of impact* [Rossi, Lipsey, and Freeman, 2004]) identify the theory or rationale behind a program and can clarify boundaries on the program's structure (Riemer and Bickman, 2011; Wholey et al., 2010). A logic model is an illustrative diagram that articulates how program resources (inputs), activities, and the direct products of those activities (outputs) are designed to produce short-term (proximal) outcomes, medium-term (distal) outcomes, and long-term impacts (Greenfield, Williams, and Eiseman, 2006; Williams et al., 2009; Knowlton and Phillips, 2013).

RAND reviewed SECO program literature and met with Military Community and Family Policy representatives, including SECO program managers, to collect the information necessary to create a SECO logic model. Illustrated in Figure 3.2, RAND applied other

Figure 3.2
RAND Logic Model of SECO Program

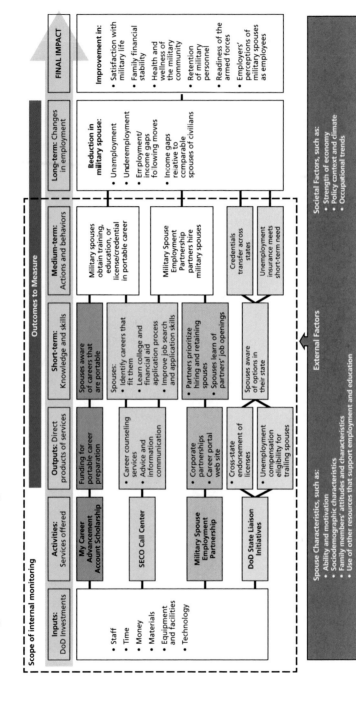

RAND RR1013-3.2

logic model designs to create a logic model that would frame the SECO program (described in Chapter Two), the outcomes SECO activities are meant to achieve, and the short-term and mediating mechanisms by which these activities are meant to support the outcomes.

Thus, this diagram can serve as a framework that Military Community and Family Policy could use to assess the degree to which this program is achieving its intended goals and to measure progress through time. It illustrates in broad terms how Military Community and Family Policy and SECO staff envision all the initiatives working together to propel change in participants' (spouses, employer partners, states) outcomes and, ultimately, how the SECO program can support community-level impacts. This figure can also help guide how an evaluation could be designed to examine the linkages across inputs, activities, outputs, and outcomes, but is not intended to model an evaluation plan or research design.

In this logic model, the **inputs** are the variety of resources, facilities, and infrastructure needed for SECO's initiatives to operate, and **activities** are the initiatives that SECO offers. A monitoring system that focused on these two elements of the logic model would address questions concerning implementation, such as:

- Did the activity receive expected resources?
- Did staff qualifications align well with the job requirements?
- Did staff sufficiently coordinate within and across the SECO program?
- Were the activities and their potential benefits well publicized among military spouses?
- Were the activities implemented as designed and within the established timeline?

The inputs and activities are designed to lead eventually to desired **impacts** on the military population depicted on the far right side of the model: improved overall satisfaction with military life, family financial stability, health and wellness of the military community, retention of military personnel, overall readiness of the armed forces, and reputation of military spouses among employers as good employees.

The logic model illustrates five measurable components of the effectiveness of the SECO program. The first is the **outputs**, which are the direct products of the services that each SECO activity provides (e.g., My Career Advancement Account Scholarship funding, SECO Call Center advice and information). One can think of outputs as data about the activities: These are the direct results of activities and are usually described in terms of the size and scope of the services (W.K. Kellogg Foundation, 2004). Output measures indicate whether a resource or service was delivered to the intended audience (e.g., eligible spouses with a need for education or career assistance) in the intended "dose" (e.g., number of career counseling sessions, amount of scholarship funding provided, type of materials distributed). Outputs are relevant indicators of spouse, employer, and state participation in SECO activities and are necessary to understand each effort's impact.

The second indicator of program effectiveness is **short-term outcomes**. These are outcomes that SECO expects its activities to affect immediately upon participation. These include specific knowledge or skills that spouses obtain by participating in a SECO activity, as well as attitudes about and awareness of the initiative. As illustrated in the logic model, one would expect that recipients of SECO Call Center career counseling would immediately obtain knowledge and insights offered by the center to assist them with their education or career goals, along with awareness of opportunities available. Military spouses who access the Military Spouse Employment Partnership Career Portal website would deepen their knowledge about job opportunities from Military Spouse Employment Partnership business partners, and partners would be better able to locate job-seeking spouses and would prioritize hiring and retaining them as employees. Concomitant attitudes about obtaining employment and education could improve.

The third component is **medium-term outcomes**. These are any changes in actions or behavior one would expect to result from the increase in awareness, knowledge, and skills and the change in attitudes produced from the short-term outcomes. The time frame for achieving these outcomes could vary, even within an initiative. For example, under the My Career Advancement Account Scholarship, one spouse might successfully obtain or renew a license for a portable career within a month of receiving the scholarship, while another might take three years to complete an associate's degree. In the logic model described, we list four possible types of medium-term outcomes, shown as they would be linked to the corresponding outputs and short-term outcomes:

1. Military spouses obtain training, education, licenses, or credentials in portable careers.
2. Military Spouse Employment Partnership partners hire military spouses.
3. Military spouses' licenses and credentials transfer across states.
4. Unemployment insurance meets the short-term need of military spouses following a military relocation.

The fourth component is **long-term outcomes**, which are the goals articulated by Military Community and Family Policy for the SECO program to address unemployment, underemployment, and income gaps. The expected **final impact**, as well, could be assessed in an evaluation, which would need to consider a realistic time frame to detect such an impact.

The key to the logic model is the dynamic flow of the relationships between and among the inputs, outputs, and outcomes. Understanding the expected connections among these components of the model will allow for systematic monitoring and evaluation so the program can undertake continuous improvements (McLaughlin and Jordan, 1999; W.K. Kellogg Foundation, 2004; Reed and Jordan; 2007; Jordan, 2010; McLaughlin and Jordan, 2010). In addition to the factors described in the logic model there are also **external factors,** outside of the control of SECO, which could affect participants' outcomes. For example, the general economic condition of the state or local region where the military family is living or relocating could affect usage rates of SECO initiatives or spouses' job opportunities. As another example, federal policies could affect the availability of jobs differently in a variety of sectors. As a hypothetical illustration, a state or local region might have fewer available positions for elementary school teachers because the federal government reduced the amount of education funding that states receive. However, that same state could have a surplus of positions available for teachers of English as a Second Language because the federal government changed the national immigration policy to allow for more family reunification visas. While no monitoring system will be able to take into consideration the entire broad array of social and economic conditions and government policies that might affect higher education, certification, or employment opportunities, any system will need to carefully consider—and prioritize—which external factors would be most relevant to consider.

Individual-level characteristics of the spouse and the service member to whom the spouse is married are other factors that may affect spouse educational and career outcomes irrespective of participation in SECO activities.. Examples of spouse characteristics include ability, motivation, preferences, number of children, previous educational attainment, and the extent to which an eligible military spouse is utilizing non-SECO loans or scholarships for his or her education (e.g., Post-911 GI Bill benefits, private or federally funded student aid and loan programs). Examples of characteristics of the military service member to whom the spouse is married that could influence spouse outcomes include education, military pay, deployment, and PCS moves. Additionally, a recent study found that serious and very serious combat injuries among service members tend to lower their spouses' labor market earnings (Heaton, Loughran, and Miller, 2012).

The proposed internal monitoring system is intended to permit managers to monitor and shape the activities, outputs, and short- or medium-term outcomes by analyzing processes, implementation, and a handful of outcomes. The dotted line in Figure 3.2 signifies the scope of an internal monitoring system. An internal monitoring system is not equipped to assess the extent to which longer-term outcomes or broader social impacts are being met, as these require a significant amount of resources and do not need to be assessed on an ongoing basis. For example, it would be important and practical to routinely monitor whether the jobs offered by Military Spouse Employment Partnership partners align with the career fields, education levels, and work experience of military spouses seeking employment through the Military Spouse Employment Partnership. Evaluating whether the Military Spouse

Employment Partnership contributes to increased military readiness and retention of service members, however, is a much more challenging and resource-intensive undertaking, and it would not be prudent to attempt to discern this on an ongoing basis. Measuring long-term outcomes and final impacts typically require additional data, manpower resources, and analyses that are beyond the scope of internal monitoring systems. Thus, measurement of effectiveness on these logic model components should take place during periodic evaluations rather than during continuous monitoring.

Step 2. Specify Indicators

Once the conceptual model of how the SECO program operates to meet intended goals has been developed, it is critical to specify key indicators that will be used to measure implementation (inputs and activities) and progress toward goals (outputs and outcomes). An indicator is a quantitative or qualitative variable that provides reliable means to measure a particular phenomenon or attribute and specifies in words or numbers a level of objective achievement, measured in terms of outcomes or tangible elements associated with project execution (Haims et al., 2011; U.S. Agency for International Development, 2009). It is important to note that a single indicator is rarely a complete measure on its own. It is important, therefore, to select multiple indicators to measure a logic model's components, implementation of activities, or progress toward goals. By using multiple indicators, the internal monitoring system can produce a more comprehensive and insightful portrait of the program.

Each component of the logic model has a corresponding type of indicator. Input indicators can assess resources necessary for operation and elements that should be in place before activities are undertaken, such as policy guidance and training of staff (Knowlton and Phillips, 2013). Process indicators are used to assess activities and how well programs are put in place and implemented. Output indicators are used to assess direct products of activities, such as work completed and specifications met. Outcome indicators are used to assess whether the objectives were met and should be collected across time to assess change over time, sustainability of that change, and impact of any program changes.

Indicators should be selected to meet SMART criteria (Doran, 1981): **S**pecific, **M**easurable, **A**ctionable or **A**ppropriate, **R**eliable, and **T**ime-bound. Each criterion should answer the following question:[1]

- **Specific**: Is the indicator clear? Does it measure what it is intended to measure (processes or progress toward SECO's goals and outcomes)?
- **Measurable**: Is it evident what data should be collected? Can the necessary information/data be obtained? Can changes in the indicator be verified?
- **Actionable or appropriate**: Does the indicator sufficiently capture progress and results? Are the time and cost requirements for data collection and analysis reasonable (i.e., do Military Community and Family Policy staff have the capacity to collect and analyze the data)? Will the information measured with this indicator be useful to others outside of Military Community and Family Policy?
- **Reliable**: Is the indicator neutral and not distorted by value judgments (by the data collector)? Is the indicator able to reflect changing circumstances or situations? Is there agreement on how the indicator should be interpreted?
- **Time-bound**: Can the indicator be collected in a reasonably timely fashion?

RAND followed SMART criteria to develop a suggested set of indicators for SECO program activities, outputs, short-term outcomes, and medium-term outcomes.[2] To create this list, we first examined Mil-

---

[1] Since Doran (1981) coined the term SMART, other authors have defined each letter in the acronym in various ways. Doran defined SMART as Specific, Measurable, Assignable, Realistic, and Time-Related. We relied on various sources to define the SMART criteria to best fit the needs of the SECO monitoring and evaluation system (e.g., Baumberger and Hewitt, 1986; Haims et al. 2011; McDavis and Hawthorne, 2006).

[2] Although information on inputs (DoD investments) also exists, cost-benefit and cost-effectiveness analyses are complex (for example, they can involve converting estimated

itary Community and Family Policy's existing data-collection sources. Table 3.1 maps where the available data sources inform *at least one* indicator for any SECO activity within each component of the logic model. An activity's appearance in a cell does not necessarily signify that the indicators available are *sufficient* for monitoring purposes, simply that at least one indicator exists.

Table 3.1 shows that Military Community and Family Policy's data sources at the time of this review had a strong foundation in collecting information for activities and outputs across the program, and for the My Career Advancement Account Scholarship in particular. However, indicators for short- and medium-term outcomes are scarce, with indicators on short-term outcomes available only for the Military Spouse Employ-

Table 3.1
Data Sources That Inform Logic Model Components for SECO Program Elements

Data Sources	Activities	Outputs	Short-Term	Medium-Term
My Career Advancement Account Scholarship data	MyCAA	MyCAA	—	MyCAA
2012 Active Duty Spouse Survey	MyCAA	MyCAA	—	—
2015 Active Duty Spouse Survey	MyCAA	MyCAA	—	—
MySECO Customer Feedback Questionnaires	MyCAA SECO Call Center MSEP	MyCAA SECO Call Center MSEP	—	—
DoD State Liaison Office data	DSLO	DSLO	—	—
Military Spouse Employment Partnership data	MSEP	MSEP	MSEP	—

NOTES: — indicates that data are not collected for that logic model component. MyCAA=My Career Advancement Account Scholarship; DSLO= DoD State Liaison Office; MSEP=Military Spouse Employment Partnership.

inputs and outcomes into current-dollar equivalents) and require advanced, specialized skills and significant resources themselves. Therefore, the collection and evaluation of inputs is more appropriate for periodic assessment by experts rather than internal, ongoing program monitoring.

ment Partnership and indicators on medium-term outcomes available only for the My Career Advancement Account Scholarship. Few indicators exist for the SECO Call Center. The DoD State Liaison Office has no individual-level spouse indicators: Its indicators relay both how state laws have changed as a result of DoD State Liaison Office services and the estimated number of spouses who live in states that have made movement toward desired changes.

RAND then analyzed in greater detail the indicators that are already collected by the Military Community Family Policy and identified which indicators do not yet exist and would need additional data collection efforts. RAND's suggested indicators and additional data collection efforts to inform the internal monitoring system are listed in Appendix A. If other initiatives are added to the SECO program, Military Community and Family Policy can augment the indicator list.

Step 3. Identify Benchmarks and Targets

Step 2 produces indicators, but managers need to understand how to measure and interpret those indicators so they can determine when or whether efforts are successful. Therefore, the indicators developed in Step 2 for outputs and outcomes should have accompanying targets for performance and benchmarks for evaluating progress or success. Typically, targets are measurable finite goals, a "desired level of performance to be reached within a specific time" (Kusek and Rist, 2014, p. 91), such as a number of Military Spouse Employment Partnership partners or number of states making unemployment insurance available to military spouses following a PCS move. Targets should be able to answer *how much* or *how many*. Without benchmarks or targets, it can be difficult to determine whether the findings from analyses represent meaningful progress toward goals (Kusek and Rist, 2004; Bamberger, 2012; U.S. Agency for International Development and Social Impact, Inc., 2013).

One approach to establishing targets is to start with the baseline measure—the previous performance—of a selected indicator, choose a desired level (or rate) of improvement of that indicator, and then examine the indicator's trend over a brief period of time. If the level or rate of improvement of the indicator meets with expectations, then the Military Community and Family Policy office can start to establish a performance target (or set of targets). If the level or rate of improvement exceeds or falls dramatically short of expected performance, the Military Community and Family Policy office can explore possible reasons why and modify targets accordingly, if necessary. Further, a target does not need to be a specific number or percentage; it could be a range (e.g., an increase of 5–10 percent within one year) (Kusek and Rist, 2004; Bamberger, 2012; U.S. Agency for International Development and Social Impact, Inc., 2013).

There are four considerations when establishing appropriate targets. One is agreement on the definition of the baseline of an indicator, based on a clear agreement regarding what previous performance includes. For example, the baseline could be an average of a certain time period's data or a snapshot of one data point. A second consideration is the level of resources and organizational capacity required to feasibly implement an initiative or program so that targets can be met. A third consideration is the timetable by which short-term or medium-term outcomes are expected to be reached. It might make sense to set interim targets that can be reached in the short term. A fourth is flexibility in setting targets: There might be external factors or shocks (for example, an economic downturn or further drawdown of troops) outside the control of staff that could affect resources or even participants' interaction with the SECO initiatives. Changes to inputs (such as budgets and staffing) might also call for target reevaluation. It is impossible to account for all possible external shocks when setting targets, but staff can adjust targets when confronted with any unexpected externalities (Kusek and Rist, 2004; Bamberger, 2012; U.S. Agency for International Development and Social Impact, Inc., 2013).

Sample targets for each SECO initiative include the following measures that could be tracked overall and by subpopulations of interest:

- the My Career Advancement Account Scholarship
  - Percentage of eligible spouses aware of the scholarships

- Percentage of users who complete their objective within the three-year window
- the SECO Call Center
  - Percentage of military spouses satisfied with SECO counseling in customer feedback questionnaire
  - Number of unique monthly visitors to SECO Call Center informational web pages
- the Military Spouse Employment Partnership
  - Number of employers becoming partners
  - Number of military spouses hired by partners
    - Overall and by common military spouse career fields and locations
- the DoD State Liaison Office
  - Number of states that have legislation in place to accept cross-state licenses for military spouses following a PCS move
  - Percentage of military spouses aware of post-PCS licensing options

Benchmarks are baselines or groups against which progress can be assessed. They should be able to answer questions about *threshold comparisons* or *comparison groups*. Benchmarks for each SECO initiative could simply be the indicator from the previous year. For example, out of the 2012 ADSS respondents who were eligible spouses who did not use the My Career Advancement Account Scholarship, 54 percent were unaware of the scholarship (Friedman, Miller, and Evans, 2015). In this example, the indicator is *awareness of the scholarship among eligible spouses*. Military Community and Family Policy could set a target, or goal, to increase awareness to 75 percent of eligible nonusers on the next ADSS. The benchmark (or comparison group used to assess progress) would be 54 percent. Thus, even if the target were not reached, increased awareness would still be an indicator of progress.

As another example for the My Career Advancement Account Scholarship, one could examine scholarship recipients' completion rates for associate's degrees or occupational certificates compared with the national average completion rate of students who have similar sociodemographic characteristics. Military spouses pursuing a degree may have characteristics similar to other married students or "nontraditional" students (those who are age 24 or older; are not pursuing higher education full time or not immediately after graduating from high school; and have family and work responsibilities, as well as other life circumstances that can interfere with successful completion of educational objectives [Advisory Committee on Student Financial Assistance, 2012]). Such characteristics could influence their decisions on whether to enroll in higher education or invest the time required to earn a degree. For example, some military spouses who receive the scholarship may not be entering higher education immediately out of high school, they may have dependents, they could be concurrently employed or pursuing their education part-time, and such events as deployments or PCS moves can disrupt their education. "Nontraditional" students typically attend higher education part-time, which has been shown to lengthen the time to completion in U.S. degree programs: Of the students enrolled in a certificate program designed to be completed in one year, 12 percent of part-time students and 28 percent of full-time students completed it within two years. Of the students enrolled in an associate's degree program designed to take two years to complete, only 8 percent of part-time students and 19 percent of full-time students completed it within four years. Of students enrolled in a bachelor's degree program designed to take four years to complete, only 25 percent of part-time students and 61 percent of full-time students completed it within eight years (Complete College America, 2011, p. 7). Using "nontraditional" students' educational outcomes could therefore be a useful and appropriate benchmark to determine whether scholarship goals are reached within a reasonable time frame.[3]

Step 4. Collect, Organize, and Visualize Data into a Monitoring Matrix

Establishing a structure for SECO managers to collect, process, organize, store, and visualize data over time is essential for creating an easy-to-use, pragmatic, and dependable internal monitoring system.

---

[3] See Buryk et al. (2015) for further discussion of how nontraditional students can serve as a useful benchmark for service members pursuing higher education.

Therefore, to maximize continuous tracking of each SECO initiative's performance, the next step is to take the data on the SMART indicators created in Step 2 alongside their accompanying targets and benchmarks created in Step 3 and collect and organize this material into a data collection template or tool, which we refer to as a *Monitoring Matrix*. In the civilian literature, this type of tool is often referred to as a *data dashboard*; it provides feedback to a user while performing a task—such as while teaching, implementing a health intervention, or managing a company (see, for example, Marsh, Pane, and Hamilton, 2006; Ikemoto and Marsh, 2006; Swan, 2009; Ryan et al., 2014; Bors et al., 2015; Krapels et al., 2015).[4]

Data should be entered at specific time intervals and reviewed on an ongoing basis. (We discuss suggested time intervals in Chapter Four). Standards for data collection and storing should be written down and easily followed, so that staff can collect data in a reliable and systematic fashion. Regular quality control checks should be put in place to ensure that data are accurate and valid.

Depending on resources available, staff expertise or other organizational constraints, the SECO Monitoring Matrix can be constructed as a relational database (e.g., Tableau) or an Excel workbook. In either case, the Monitoring Matrix is not a static data collector, but a data analysis and visualization tool. This tool will allow SECO staff to analyze the data in various ways, as deemed appropriate. Table 3.2 and Figure 3.3 illustrate how the Monitoring Matrix could work in practice for the My Career Advancement Account Scholarship. Table 3.2 lists the relevant data and data sources needed to monitor the sample question: *Is the My Career Advancement Account Scholarship reaching military spouses in need?*

---

[4] We intentionally choose not to use the term *dashboard* in the SECO internal monitoring system. In the military setting, leaders typically use a dashboard to provide them with input on the status of performance of an operation or program's set of indicators, with a color code of red where there are problems, yellow where there are emerging or dissipating issues, and green where indicators are in the acceptable range. While the use of indicators to inform decisionmaking is similar in both cases, the Monitoring Matrix is different in that we do not suggest that all of the indicators need to be continuously color-coded.

Table 3.2
Example Monitoring Matrix Indicators Needed to Examine "Is the My Career Advancement Account Scholarship Reaching Military Spouses in Need?"

Indicators	Data Sources
Number of spouses demographically eligible for MyCAA	Defense Enrollment Eligibility Reporting System
Number of successful account registrations for scholarship	Program data
Number of applications for scholarship	Program data

Data to address this question include account registrations and applications for scholarships. These data would be combined with data describing the sociodemographic characteristics of the population of users and eligible users to determine the rate of participation in different aspects of the process (e.g., applying for a scholarship, seeking information). These rates would reflect a combination of factors, such as spouse awareness of the scholarship, whether the scholarship fills a need, and whether the spouse is able to take advantage of the

Figure 3.3
Fictitious Visualization of MySECO Portal Activity Tracking

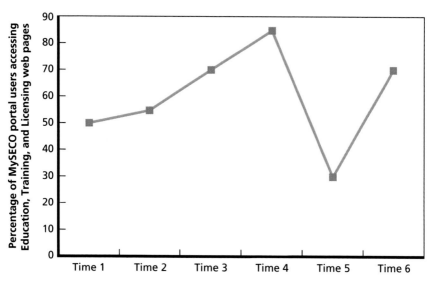

opportunity at that point in time.[5] The data to make these calculations will come from different sources. Internal data sources (initiative data or data from the MySECO portal) could be updated on a monthly basis and fed into the Monitoring Matrix. Estimates of the number of spouses potentially eligible for the scholarship, drawn from the Defense Enrollment Eligibility Reporting System (DEERS) in which all military service members' dependents must enroll to be eligible for benefits), could be updated on an annual basis because this number should not show extreme variations in shorter time frames. Each year, Military Community and Family Policy publishes demographic reports on the military community (see, for example, Office of the Deputy Assistant Secretary of Defense for Military Community and Family Policy, 2014). With minor variation to figures already included in these reports, Military Community and Family Policy could obtain tables of spouses' and service member sponsors' sociodemographic characteristics, thereby determining by pay grade the number of married active component military personnel whose spouses are not active component military personnel. Note these data can serve only as a measure of spouses' *potential eligibility*, because DEERS can identify only spouse and service member demographic characteristics—not whether spouses' education and/or career goals would be eligible for My Career Advancement Account Scholarship funding.

Figure 3.3 illustrates the possible graphic visualization that could be achieved using fictitious data for an example calculation: *(Number of unique users accessing Education, Training, and Licensing web pages on MySECO portal)÷(Number of unique users of MySECO portal).*

SECO program staff might want to explore why the percentage of MySECO portal users dropped to 30 percent at Time Point 5. For example, if the proportion of users of other SECO portal web pages did not change as dramatically at the same points in time, then SECO

---

[5] Competing obligations may necessitate postponement of pursuit of educational opportunities. In the 2012 ADSS, 79 percent of eligible spouses who were aware of the My Career Advancement Account Scholarship and believed they were eligible indicated that they did not use a My Career Advancement Account Scholarship in the previous year because family or personal obligations limited their time to pursue education or training (Friedman, Miller, and Evans, 2015, p. 27).

program staff would be able to see that the changes were unique to the Education, Training, and Licensing web pages, and further exploration as to why the changes were occurring might be warranted. It might be that the Education, Training, and Licensing web page was being updated at that time point, so few people were able to access it, or it could be that the web page was not perceived to be useful by users (as determined through Customer Feedback Questionnaire results). Depending on the benchmarks or targets developed in Step 3 and the number of spouses affected, SECO staff could determine whether changes over time were meaningful or practically significant.

Figure 3.4 offers another example of how indicators listed in the Monitoring Matrix can be visualized and therefore used for internal decisionmaking. Here, we ask the question to measure a medium-term outcome for SECO: *Do spouses find SECO resources to be helpful for finding a job?* To answer this question, we would use data from the Customer Feedback Questionnaire administered three to six months after initial contact with a SECO Counselor. Spouses who report being employed at the time of the follow-up survey are asked about whether they are working, and if so, "How helpful were the resources available at the MySECO website or your career counselor in finding your job?" Response options are "very helpful," "somewhat helpful," and "not at all helpful." For a fictitious example, Figure 3.4 presents data over three separate, contiguous data pulls. This could be done once a week, once a month, or once a quarter, for example.

In this example, Military Community Family Policy could note that the perceived helpfulness of the MySECO website or career counselors was much lower among respondents who were employed full-time (98 percent responded "not at all") in the first time period that the data were examined (Data Pull 1) compared with the other time periods. SECO staff could then consider whether these reflect seasonal fluctuations or national unemployment trends, but also check in with career counselors about whether they have observed any changes in the types of spouses seeking help or the types of help that spouses are seeking. This same type of figure could be used to observe whether any identifiable change follows revisions to counseling designed to help spouses obtain full-time rather than part-time or temporary work. Similar figures also

Figure 3.4
Fictitious Visualization of SECO Medium-Term Outcomes: Helpfulness in Finding a Job

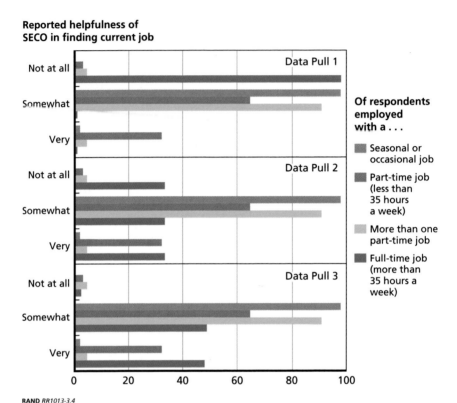

RAND RR1013-3.4

could be used to track such things as helpfulness of SECO resources for spouses according to whether they report on the Customer Feedback Questionnaire that their current job makes use of their skills, training, or experience (a great deal, somewhat, not at all), or whether they are satisfied with their current job (a great deal, somewhat, not at all).

Each outcome could also be examined for different subgroups of military spouses. Figure 3.5 illustrates the same question as Figure 3.4, but only for respondents who are employed full-time, separated by rank of a spouse's service member: junior enlisted, noncommissioned officers, junior officers, and senior officers. Figure 3.5 shows an alternate layout for this information as well: Military Community and Family

Figure 3.5
Fictitious Visualization of SECO Medium-Term Outcome: Helpfulness in Finding a Full-Time Job, by Spouse Sponsor's Rank

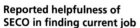

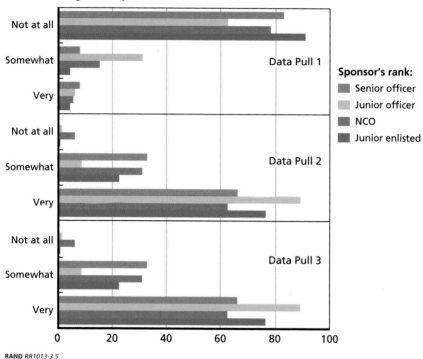

RAND RR1013-3.5

Policy can format the information according to its own preferences. It might be useful to understand whether the perceived helpfulness of SECO resources varies among spouses with service member sponsors of different ranks, and therefore varied education level and years of experience that might also help facilitate a job search. In this fictional example, we see that in Data Pull 1, many of the spouses, regardless of service member's rank, found the SECO resources "not at all" helpful. Reports then improved: In Data Pulls 2 and 3, more respondents reported that the resources were "very" helpful. Based on this fictitious data from Figures 3.4 and 3.5, staff could examine whether any issues with the website occurred in the time period directly prior to Data

Pull 1, other issues arose with the quality or capacity of counselors, or there were external shocks like the 2008 economic downturn. They also could determine whether further study was needed to uncover other operational issues at hand.

Investing in the capability to visualize data organized into the Monitoring Matrix also would provide staff with the ability to document a wide range of metrics and indicators over time in a fast, reliable, and easy-to-read format to compare changes within and across initiatives.

Appendix A of this report provides specific indicators that Military Community and Family Policy can include in its Monitoring Matrix for current initiatives, as well as data sources from which Military Community and Family Policy can pull the indicators. As an example of the indicators and data sources a Monitoring Matrix can warehouse, examine Table A.1 in Appendix A. The first column lists the SECO logic model component (activities, outputs, short-term outcomes, and medium-term outcomes) for which an indicator or set of indicators can measure. Subsequent columns list suggested indicators organized by the data source from which they can be drawn. My Career Advancement Account Scholarship indicators listed in Table A.1 can be provided through a number of data sources (organized into columns two through six): program data, responses on the Active Duty Survey of Spouses, information from a user feedback questionnaire, data on number of visitors to MySECO Portal, and responses on the MySECO Portal Customer Feedback Questionnaire (described in more detail below).

Step 5. Using Data to Inform Decisionmaking for Ongoing Improvements

The ultimate purpose of an internal monitoring system is to enable program administrators to answer questions about program functioning and monitor progress toward program goals. Thus, program managers can identify negative trends that call for further investigation and look for desirable and undesirable changes following a program or policy modifications in a more timely manner than periodic evaluations permit. Internal monitoring is a dynamic process that requires an iterative cycle of assessment of collected data to determine whether SECO initiatives are functioning as designed and providing optimum support to spouses—and if not, where efforts can be improved. To distill the wide range of information organized in the Monitoring Matrix to inform decisionmaking (Step 5), this section outlines a process by which Military Community and Family Policy can assess performance and manage its SECO program.

Using data collected, analyzed, and visualized through the Monitoring Matrix, Military Community and Family Policy can assess whether SECO initiatives are "doing the work in the right way," in terms of implementation. That is, staff can track whether processes are operating as expected. Military Community and Family Policy also can manage the SECO program in a way to ensure that that SECO initiatives are "doing the right work," in terms of whether activities are producing expected outputs and activities are meeting intended short- or medium-term outcomes.

Core questions that should be asked from analysis drawn from the Monitoring Matrix data include:

- What happened in the past period?
  - Were processes implemented as designed?
  - Are expected outputs occurring?
  - Are short- and medium-term outcomes being met? How does this compare to benchmarks or targets?

If the tracking of trends through the Monitoring Matrix suggests that processes are not operating as expected or goals are not being met, Military Community and Family Policy will need to ask a series of questions to determine why this is the case. This could require more-extensive analysis than SECO staff has the capacity to undertake, suggesting a third-party evaluator might need to be contracted.

Core questions that should be asked from analysis drawn from the Monitoring Matrix data include:

- If goals were not met, is further study or inquiry required to determine why?
  - Are there external factors that need to be considered?

- Do other partners need to be included to improve meeting goals?
- Do benchmarks or targets need adjustment?

In addition to following short- or medium-term outcomes on a regular basis, Monitoring Matrix information can enable periodic evaluations of longer-term outcomes, such as spouse unemployment rates or retention of married service members. A number of questions to further assess the performance of the SECO efforts as related to longer-term outcomes include:

- Is the current slate of SECO activities sufficiently designed to meet the needs of military spouses and eventually meet the longer-term goals?
  - If not, which needs are not being met?
  - How does programming need to shift to address them?
  - What are the hurdles, gaps, or redundancies?
- If the design of the current program is appropriate, do the processes need to be tweaked?
- Do benchmarks or targets need to be modified to be more realistic or feasible?

Conclusion

This chapter outlined the five steps in developing a rigorous and practical internal monitoring system for the SECO program: (1) articulate a logic model to frame the conceptual model of how each initiative is expected to meet SECO strategic goals; (2) develop SMART indicators to correspond with each component of the logic model; (3) craft benchmarks and targets to correspond with each indicator so that progress can be measured against expected performance; (4) collect, organize, analyze, and visualize the data through a Monitoring Matrix; and (5) use the data and analysis from the Monitoring Matrix to assess and manage the SECO program and inform decisionmaking for continual improvements. Internal monitoring is not without its challenges. In the next chapter, we recommend practical suggestions to support the implementation of the SECO internal monitoring system.

CHAPTER FOUR

Implementation of the SECO Internal Monitoring System

There are several challenges to implementing and maintaining the proposed SECO internal monitoring system. First, to measure progress on all components of the SECO logic model, additional indicators will need to be identified and collected through either new or existing data sources. Second, staff will need to select appropriate benchmarks or targets to adequately measure progress of each indicator. Third, staff capacity and technological systems will need to be put in place to ensure that the Monitoring Matrix is useful and provides the necessary information to support decisionmaking. Fourth, mileposts or reflection points will need to be built into staff schedules so that adequate attention is given to using the internal monitoring system to assess and manage the SECO program.

Collect Sufficient Data to Include All Suggested Indicators

As noted under Step 2 in Chapter Three, RAND analysis found that, to date, Military Community and Family Policy has focused data collection to measure indicators of activities and outputs, but gaps remain in data on short-term or medium-term outcomes. Appendix A lists the indicators that are currently available and those that require additional or modified data collection efforts, which would greatly expand the indicators available to inform the monitoring system. For most of the additional indicators listed in Appendix A, further data collection would come through three mechanisms: additional questions asked in the ADSS, a future My Career Advancement Account

Scholarship–initiated customer feedback questionnaire, and RAND's proposed follow-up module added to the MySECO portal Customer Feedback Questionnaire currently administered to voluntary users of the MySECO portal for internal quality assurance purposes. In the future, Military Community and Family Policy plans to integrate the My Career Advancement Account Scholarship, the Military Spouse Employment Partnership, and the MySECO web portals so that a spouse using these websites will have one record associated with him or her across the initiatives.

Next, we describe recommended additions or modifications to the ADSS and the Customer Feedback Questionnaire.

Suggested additional questions for ADSS. The ADSS is conducted by the Human Resources Strategic Assessment Program at DMDC. As noted in Table 3.1, the ADSS contains information that is relevant for monitoring short- and medium-term outcomes for the My Career Advancement Account Scholarship. The 2012 ADSS was administered from November 2012 to March 2013 and had a 23-percent response rate, with about 12,000 respondents from the four services. DMDC began administering the 2015 ADSS in December 2014. Both the 2012 and 2015 ADSS include questions assessing spouses' awareness of the My Career Advancement Account Scholarship, their use of a My Career Advancement Account, and their perceived barriers to using it (DMDC 2013, 2015). The 2015 ADSS asks whether the respondent is in school or training—and, if so, the reason for pursuing higher education. It also asks whether the respondent has utilized SECO Call Center education and career counseling in the past six months and the extent to which he or she found it useful. We propose further leveraging the ADSS to provide additional information that would be useful in monitoring both the My Career Advancement Account Scholarship and other SECO initiatives. These additions would be aimed at answering key questions about program take-up and use among military spouses. For example, additional items could measure the reasons why military spouses use SECO and these data could be used to inform program design and implementation. Is it to prepare for a first career or a career change? Is it to improve job search and application skills? Are they seeking assistance in selecting, applying for, and funding a course of study in higher education? To find employers who are hiring military spouses? Do the reasons for using SECO change over time? Do spouses who receive a scholarship for portable career training also use other SECO resources for career preparation and job searches? These additions would greatly enhance Military Community and Family Policy's ability to understand its customers' reasons for using the SECO program.

The indicator list in Appendix A includes the ADSS as a data source. RAND-suggested questions to add to ADSS are listed there.

Suggested additional follow-up module for the MySECO Customer Feedback Questionnaire. At the time of this study, Military Community and Family Policy offers MySECO portal users the opportunity to comment on their level of satisfaction and perceived usefulness of the website and the online or telephone counseling they are provided. Representatives report that MySECO counselors typically field 10,000 calls a month from military spouses. After each encounter with a counselor, spouses are asked to complete a customer feedback questionnaire. Each month, approximately 26 percent of spouse users of the MySECO portal complete this questionnaire. Military Community and Family Policy receives monthly snapshot reports on the comments that spouses provide through this feedback tool. The feedback provided on this questionnaire can be helpful for identifying areas for improvement (e.g., where spouses express dissatisfaction), but the results should not be interpreted as though this were a scientific survey using sampling and weighting strategies to obtain a representative set of results. To illustrate, if 20 percent of spouses on the Customer Feedback Questionnaire indicate that a SECO online support resource they used was not helpful for them, Military Community and Family Policy cannot conclude that 20 percent of all spouses who used the resource felt that way. It can, however, investigate the responses of those who were unsatisfied to explore whether certain types of material might be lacking from that website, a link to that information is broken, the information is outdated, it is difficult to locate, or is not be presented in a clear manner, etc.

To provide a deeper understanding on whether services provided are resulting in users' improved short-term and medium-term outcomes as defined in the SECO logic model, Military Community and Family Policy started in September 2015 to administer two sets of additional questions to Customer Feedback Questionnaire respondents who voluntarily agree to participate. The purpose of the additional questions is to elicit detailed information about specific types of SECO activities from MySECO Customer Feedback Questionnaire respondents.

The first set is offered to all respondents immediately following their completion of the MySECO Customer Feedback Questionnaire and gathers information on respondents' education and employment goals, initiative outputs, and short-term outcomes. Questions assess the status of respondents' careers or educational plans or efforts, as well as use of and satisfaction with SECO initiatives. For example, questions about education goals inquire whether the spouse used the MySECO website or their career counselor to help them choose a field of study, degree, or program, and how helpful those resources were in making this choice.

The second set of questions will be offered to respondents three to six months later. The follow-up questionnaire respondents will be made up of volunteers who consented to receiving the follow-up questionnaire and provided an email address upon completion of the MySECO Portal Customer Feedback Questionnaire. These volunteers are contacted via email between three and six months after completion of the initial feedback questionnaire and are given a link to the follow-up questionnaire. The questionnaire is designed to gather information on medium-term outcomes. Respondents will be asked about their experience applying for and using the My Career Advancement Account Scholarship (if applicable), their current education status, and their use of and satisfaction with the MySECO website and their career counselor. Employment questions will ask about the status of spouses' career searches, including whether they have applied for jobs or interviewed with Military Spouse Employment Partnership employers and whether they have been able to successfully transfer a job-related state license or certificate (if applicable).

Appendix B contains the RAND-suggested items for the two sets of questions.

Accompany Selected Indicators with Meaningful Benchmarks or Targets

Step 3 of the SECO internal monitoring system is the development of benchmarks or targets to accompany each indicator. This step is vital for staff to determine what is reasonable and meaningful progress. The development of benchmarks or targets should take into consideration any external factors (as delineated at the bottom of the SECO logic model). External factors, such as economic downturns or improvements, military manpower fluctuations, or major federal and state employment or education policy changes, could have an impact on SECO program outcomes. They could lead to changes in military spouse behaviors and attitudes that have nothing to do with the quality of the SECO programming. For example, a marked decrease in the number of My Career Advancement Account Scholarship users could potentially be explained by a large troop drawdown or an improvement in the job market and not necessarily a decline in quality, awareness, or accessibility of the scholarship.

Support Military Community and Family Policy Staff Capacity

A key mechanism to ensure that an internal monitoring system will be useful and relevant is to ensure that SECO staff are aware of the need for the system, are included in discussions about the indicators and development of benchmarks or targets, and are trained to use the technology needed to employ the Monitoring Matrix as a useful tool for analysis. SECO staff should use the questions and examples provided in Table 3.2 to create their own benchmarks and targets for each indicator listed in Appendix A or developed in the future.

Furthermore, SECO staff should communicate clearly with the contractors who are currently tasked with continuous data collection (e.g., program data or Customer Feedback Questionnaires for internal quality assurance) so that data can be collected in a timely fashion and are reliable, valid, and error-free. One option to ensure that contractor-collected data are provided to Military Community and Family Policy and aggregated in a consistent time frame would be to automate data uploads to the Monitoring Matrix (e.g., data analysis software can be programed to output indicator data into spreadsheets). To be clear, we are referring here to ongoing data collection by the SECO program vendors, not the periodic ADSS or other types of information such as dates of state legislative changes.

Establish Regular Reflection Points

For the SECO internal monitoring system to be useful, regular mileposts should be established, at which point reviews of Monitoring Matrix visualizations and analyses would be reviewed and decisions for assessing SECO program performance or management could be made. Without regular reflection points, the internal monitoring system will lose its utility and could become a stagnant data collection effort, rather than an exercise to support decisionmaking that will maximize the ongoing impact of the SECO program. At specific milestone points (e.g., quarterly, annually), SECO staff should review the data collected on each indicator and compare progress with determined benchmarks or targets.

The timing of the reflection points does not have to be the same for all SECO initiatives; rather, it could be based on already-determined cycles of data flow to Military Community and Family Policy, initiative needs, or fixed time points. Some questions to support the timing of reflection points are the following:

- *How frequently are data typically available? What are key milestones in the activities?*
  - The Customer Feedback Questionnaire is administered on an ongoing, voluntary basis to spouses who use the services on the MySECO portal. These data are then shared with Military Community and Family Policy on a monthly basis. Military Community and Family Policy may therefore decide to reflect on Customer Feedback Questionnaire data when it arrives or determine that less frequent reviews are sufficient if a small

number of spouses (e.g., fewer than 25) complete the questionnaire each month.
- My Career Advancement Account Scholarship education institutions need to provide Military Community and Family
  Policy with data on enrollment each term so that funds can be
  transferred to the institution. Therefore, a reflection point each
  term and when grades are released might make sense.
- ADSS data have a more obvious reflection point, as the survey
  is administered approximately every other year. Therefore,
  Military Community and Family Policy can review the ADSS
  results once DMDC provides them.
- *How much data are available at any given time?*
  - If an initiative is collecting data from only a few spouses at a
    time, having a relatively long period (e.g., one year) between
    reflection points could be feasible.
  - Conversely, if an initiative is collecting data from a large number
    of spouses at short intervals, then waiting too long between
    reflection points might not allow for timely decisionmaking.
- *Are there any pressing issues that need to be addressed immediately
  or continually?*
  - Reflection points could be scheduled to follow up after an anal-
    ysis of any concerning trends or results. For example, although
    complaints or grievances submitted through the Customer
    Feedback Questionnaire or the DoD Complaint System are not
    necessarily representative of all military spouses' experiences,
    they could showcase an immediate or most troubling problem.
    Taking action to remedy the problem, and then reviewing the
    data on a frequent basis, could support active response to press-
    ing issues.
- *Are there any major decisions that require a one-off reflection or
  review?*
  - It would be prudent to schedule a major review of data well in
    advance of any major budget or policy decisions.
  - Congressional calls for data or testimony could require Mili-
    tary Community and Family Policy to review data outside of
    the regularly scheduled reflection points.

While it might seem to provide a certain efficiency during the reflection points to review only the data from the initiative that is under review at the time, incorporating recent information from other SECO initiatives could provide additional context and an overall richer picture of broad trends in military spouse education and employment.

Conclusion

This document has outlined a suggested strategy for the DoD's Military Community and Family Policy to establish an internal monitoring system for its SECO program. RAND developed this guidance by applying the knowledge base reflected in literature on program evaluation and performance measurement to support Military Community and Family Policy's SECO program, which focus on the education and employment of military spouses. These initiatives include career counseling services available through the SECO Call Center at Military OneSource; scholarships for testing, education, and training for portable career fields through the My Career Advancement Account Scholarship; avenues to connect spouses with potential employers through the Military Spouse Employment Partnership; and DoD State Liaison Office efforts to improve the portability of occupational licenses and credentials across state lines and to expand unemployment compensation eligibility to military spouses following their service member's PCS move.

Development of the internal monitoring system involved developing a logic model for the SECO program, using SMART criteria to specify structured indicators to measure the goals and objectives outlined in the logic model, detailing guidelines for developing indicator targets and benchmarks, and organizing indicators, targets, and benchmarks into a Monitoring Matrix. Finally, we outlined the challenges to implementing and maintaining the proposed internal monitoring system and suggested steps to address these challenges.

It is important to note that the guidance provided in this document is meant to inform an internal monitoring system, rather than a formal evaluation. Although evaluations and internal monitoring are both systematic processes for understanding program functioning—and both processes provide information that can help inform decisions, improve performance, and achieve planned results—there are important distinctions between the two methods. Internal monitoring is designed to provide constant and continual feedback on the progress of a program, and is typically conducted by program staff. In contrast, evaluations are done independently, typically by an external body, are more rigorous in their methodology and analysis, and aim to provide program managers with an objective assessment of the extent to which a program produced the intended outcomes and impacts.

In addition to helping the office of Military Community and Family Policy monitor the array of SECO initiatives it administers, the guidance provided within this report can also be useful to other government entities or organizations confronted with the challenge of managing programs and identifying and assessing metrics of progress.

RAND-Suggested Indicators for a SECO Internal Monitoring System

This appendix displays RAND's suggested indicators for the SECO internal monitoring system. Separate tables are provided for each initiative: the My Career Advancement Account Scholarship, the SECO Call Center, the Military Spouse Employment Partnership, and the DoD State Liaison Office.

Indicators are organized by the logic model component in which they fall and by data source. Within each table are some indicators that Military Community and Family Policy already measures and uses to track progress (e.g., number of Military Spouse Employment Partnership partners and number of states that provide unemployment compensation to trailing military spouses). In some cases, the data may be available but not typically used to track progress.

Indicators for which additional data collection would be needed are bolded. Some cells were intentionally left blank because an indicator in a different cell measured that logic model component more appropriately or more feasibly.

The ADSS is one data source listed in each table. We recognize that the survey could collect a lot of information about SECO initiatives. However, because this survey collects information from spouses on myriad topics and should remain a reasonable length to increase the likelihood that spouses will answer all the questions, we have not listed all potential indicators within these tables. Instead, we have prioritized the most-pressing indicators that could be collected through the ADSS.

Table A.1
RAND-Suggested My Career Advancement Account Scholarship Indicators

Logic Model Components and Associated Questions	Data Source				
	MyCAA Scholarship Data	Active Duty Spouse Survey	MyCAA-Initiated Feedback Questionnaire[a]	MySECO Portal	MySECO Portal Customer Feedback Questionnaire
Activities					
Is the scholarship reaching the desired target populations; i.e., military spouses in need? Are eligible and interested military spouses using this SECO activity?	Number of account registrations for the My Career Advancement Account Scholarship Proportion of eligible spouses that created an account Proportion of accounts recently used	Respondent knowledge of the My Career Advancement Account Reasons for respondent's use of the My Career Advancement Account Scholarship to pursue higher education • To advance career • To increase earnings potential • Self-fulfillment/ intellectual curiosity • No employment opportunities at my current education level • No employment opportunities in my current career field			Number of users of MySECO Portal interested in the My Career Advancement Account Scholarship

Table A.1—Continued

Logic Model Components and Associated Questions	MyCAA Scholarship Data	Active Duty Spouse Survey	MyCAA-Initiated Feedback Questionnaire[a]	MySECO Portal	MySECO Portal Customer Feedback Questionnaire
			Data Source		
How usable and useful are the resources—e.g., website?	Information distribution about the scholarship (# of web ads, pamphlets, etc.) Number of phone calls counselors return within three days Social media presence: Number of users and links on Facebook and LinkedIn		**Clarity and usability of information on website (interface) and application process, registration**	Number of web page hits Number of up-to-date pages/links on the My Career Advancement Account Scholarship website Account registrations for MySECO portal	
Is length of scholarship funding availability (three years) sufficient to meet military spouses' needs?	Number of waivers requested Number of waivers at the three-year limit approved				

Table A.1—Continued

Logic Model Components and Associated Questions	Data Source				
	MyCAA Scholarship Data	Active Duty Spouse Survey	MyCAA-Initiated Feedback Questionnaire[a]	MySECO Portal	MySECO Portal Customer Feedback Questionnaire
Outputs					
Are services of high quality? Are spouses getting the resources they need to receive training for portable careers?	Length of time for an education or training plan to be approved Average number of days/hours for spouse to talk to consultants after calling Number of applications approved Proportion of military spouses awarded scholarships who use them Number and percentage of schools whose grade submissions are past due		**Satisfaction with the My Career Advancement Account Scholarship information available on MySECO web portal**		Satisfaction with the My Career Advancement Account Scholarship information available on MySECO Portal

Table A.1—Continued

Logic Model Components and Associated Questions	Data Source				
	MyCAA Scholarship Data	Active Duty Spouse Survey	MyCAA-Initiated Feedback Questionnaire[a]	MySECO Portal	MySECO Portal Customer Feedback Questionnaire
Short-term outcomes					
Are spouses aware of careers that are portable?			**Spouses' reports that information available on the My Career Advancement Account Scholarship Portal has improved their awareness of careers that are portable**		
Medium-term outcomes					
Are trained spouses able to establish their careers?	Number of degrees/certificates awarded by career field; **Participants' rates of continuing from one year to the next in higher education**	**Users' perspectives of whether the scholarship supported their career objectives**; **Whether participating spouses obtained a job upon graduation**			Users' perspectives of whether the scholarship supported their education and career objectives

NOTE: Indicators that are **bolded** require additional data collection efforts. If data on participants' characteristics can be collected, differences in outputs and outcomes by specific subgroup populations can be tracked. Suggested subgroup populations include gender, race/ethnicity, age, education level, service branch of service member sponsor, and rank or pay grade of service member sponsor.

[a] The My Career Advancement Account-Initiated Feedback Questionnaire would also require additional data collection efforts; the questionnaire does not yet exist.

Table A.2
RAND-Suggested SECO Call Center Indicators

Logic Model Components and Associated Questions	Data Source			
	SECO Call Center Data from Military OneSource	Active Duty Spouse Survey	MySECO Portal	MySECO Portal Customer Feedback Questionnaire
Activities				
Does the call center have the needed capacity to help spouses? Is the call center reaching the desired target populations?	Usage: Number of calls and emails fielded per month by: • Pillar • Resources provided	Spouse knowledge of the SECO Call Center and career counseling options	Number of web page hits; Number of clicks; Account registrations for MySECO portal	Applications for non-DoD financial aid (grants and scholarships)
Outputs				
Are the resources of high quality? Are spouses getting the resources they need to receive training for portable careers?	Counselor provides feedback on resume; Counselor helps with non-DoD grant or scholarship applications			Satisfaction with information available on MySECO Portal; Satisfaction with career counseling
Short-term outcomes				
Are military spouses learning the knowledge and skills they need to obtain desired education or employment?	Number of spouses using self-assessment tools			Average helpfulness ratings of self-assessment tools; Number of spouses identifying a career; User's perspective of whether counseling provided knowledge and skills to support education objectives; Number of spouses revising resume; Number of spouses attributing change in career field to information on MySECO website or career counseling

Table A.2—Continued

Logic Model Components and Associated Questions	Data Source			
	SECO Call Center Data from Military OneSource	Active Duty Spouse Survey	MySECO Portal	MySECO Portal Customer Feedback Questionnaire
Medium-term outcomes:				
Do the activities result in the desired outcomes? Are spouses able to establish their careers after obtaining career counseling?				Extent to which spouse attributes SECO career counseling to supporting their education or employment goals Number of job applications submitted in past month Number of spouses obtaining job interviews Number of spouses who submit applications for further education Number of spouses reporting hires after interviews Number of non-DoD grants and scholarships awarded

NOTE: Indicators that are **bolded** require additional data collection efforts. If data on participants' characteristics can be collected, differences in outputs and outcomes by specific subgroup populations can be tracked. Suggested subgroup populations include gender, race/ethnicity, age, education level, service branch of service member sponsor, and rank or pay grade of service member sponsor.

Table A.3
RAND-Suggested Military Spouse Employment Partnership Indicators

Logic Model Components and Associated Questions	Data Source			
	Partner Directory (and via Quarterly Questionnaire Fielded to Partners)[a]	Active Duty Spouse Survey	The Military Spouse Employment Partnership Career Portal	MySECO Portal Customer Feedback Questionnaire
Activities				
Does the partnership have the needed capacity to help spouses? Is the partnership reaching the desired target populations?	Number of partners Types of partners by: • Industry sector • Federal government/ private sector/ nonprofit • Types of jobs offered (full-time/part-time/ telework) • When became a partner **Whether partner offers on-the-job training, internships, tuition assistance, continuing education or other career education or training**	**Spouse knowledge of the Military Spouse Employment Partnership**	Number of web page visits Number of account registrations for career portal Number of posted job openings on career portal	Number of users of MySECO Portal interested in the Military Spouse Employment Partnership

Table A.3—Continued

Logic Model Components and Associated Questions	Data Source			
	Partner Directory (and via Quarterly Questionnaire Fielded to Partners)[a]	Active Duty Spouse Survey	The Military Spouse Employment Partnership Career Portal	MySECO Portal Customer Feedback Questionnaire
Outputs				
Are resources of high quality? Are spouses getting the resources they need to connect with partners? Is the partnership obtaining data needed from contractors? Are the data valid?	**Engagement level of partners**		Diversity of jobs offered, categorized by: • Company industry (note: not occupation) • Geographic location of positions • Temporary/part-time/full-time • Salary and seniority • **Alignment with portable careers popular among My Career Advancement Account Scholarship participants** • **Provision of on-the-job training/tuition assistance**	Average satisfaction rating with the Military Spouse Employment Partnership Rating on variety of jobs posted to meet their needs

Table A.3—Continued

Logic Model Components and Associated Questions	Data Source			
	Partner Directory (and via Quarterly Questionnaire Fielded to Partners)[a]	Active Duty Spouse Survey	The Military Spouse Employment Partnership Career Portal	MySECO Portal Customer Feedback Questionnaire
Short-term outcomes				
Do spouses know about jobs available through partners?		Extent to which spouse knows of the Military Spouse Employment Partnership career portal and jobs available		Number of spouse applications to partners
Medium-term outcomes				
Do partners hire military spouses? Are spouses able to establish their careers?	**Number of spouses interviewing with partners** Number of spouses hired by MSEP corporate partners (monthly reports)	Extent to which spouse attributes partnership to supporting employment goals		Number of spouses interviewing with partners Number of spouses reporting hires with partners after interviews

NOTE: Indicators that are **bolded** require additional data collection efforts. If data on participants' characteristics can be collected, differences in outputs and outcomes by specific subgroup populations can be tracked. Suggested subgroup populations include gender, race/ethnicity, age, education-level, service branch of service member sponsor, and rank or pay grade of service member sponsor.
[a] The quarterly questionnaire fielded to partners would also require additional data collection efforts; the questionnaire does not yet exist.

Table A.4
RAND-Suggested DoD State Liaison Office Indicators

Logic Model Components and Associated Questions	Data Source			
	DoD State Liaison Office Data	Active Duty Spouse Survey	State and DMDC Data	MySECO Portal Customer Feedback Questionnaire
Activities				
Does the office have the needed capacity to help spouses? Is the office reaching the desired target populations?	Number of states offering spouses with occupational licenses or credentials at least one of the following after a PCS move: • Obtainable endorsement • Temporary license • Expedited license Number of states that provide unemployment compensation to trailing military spouses	Spouse knowledge of the DoD State Liaison Office options for unemployment insurance, cross-state license transfer	Percentage of spouses applying for unemployment benefits out of those moving to states that offer this benefit	Number of users of MySECO Portal interested in license or certificate transfers; in unemployment compensation Number of spouses applying for license or certificate transfers
Outputs				
Is initiative making progress expanding the number of states that adopt these SECO goals?	Number of states that adopt SECO goals			

Table A.4—Continued

Logic Model Components and Associated Questions	Data Source				
	DoD State Liaison Office Data	Active Duty Spouse Survey	State and DMDC Data	MySECO Portal Customer Feedback Questionnaire	
Short-term outcomes					
Are spouses aware of the opportunities in their state (cross-state license transfer or unemployment insurance)?		**Spouses report knowledge about opportunities in their state (cross-state license transfer or unemployment insurance)**			
Medium-term outcomes					
Are spouses able to minimize career disruption following a PCS move?		**Extent to which spouse attributes cross-state license transfer or unemployment insurance with minimizing employment disruption and/or income gaps following PCS moves**		Number of spouses who transferred license with move and got a license-relevant job Percentage of spouses receiving unemployment benefits out of those moving to states that offer this benefit	

NOTE: Indicators that are **bolded** require additional data collection efforts. If data on participants' characteristics can be collected, differences in outputs and outcomes by specific subgroup populations can be tracked. Suggested subgroup populations include gender, race/ethnicity, age, education level, service branch of service member sponsor, and rank or pay grade of service member sponsor.

RAND Suggested Additions to the MySECO Portal Customer Feedback Questionnaire

This appendix includes the questions suggested by RAND to add to the Military Community and Family Policy's MySECO Portal Customer Feedback Questionnaire. The purpose of RAND's suggested additional questions is to elicit detailed information about specific types of SECO activities from MySECO Customer Feedback Questionnaire respondents. This information will provide a deeper understanding for the Military Community and Family Policy office on whether services provided through the MySECO web portal are resulting in users' improved short- and medium-term outcomes, as defined in the SECO logic model.

The first set includes questions asked to military spouses upon their completion of the MySECO Portal Customer Feedback Questionnaire. The second set is a series of follow-up questions asked to volunteer military spouses who agree to complete another questionnaire three to six months later.

RAND's Suggested Additional Questions for the MySECO Customer Feedback Questionnaire

1. Thinking about the past year, which of the following statements best applies to you? (check one)
   a. I have been **gathering information** about enrolling in a college (including community college), university, or trade school, **but I am not planning on applying to a program right now**.
   b. I have been **gathering information** about enrolling in a college (including community college), university, or trade school, **and I am planning on applying to a program this coming year**.
   c. I have applied to a degree or licensing program (including community colleges, four-year colleges and universities, or trade schools), **but I have not been accepted yet**.
   d. I **applied** to a degree or licensing program (including community colleges, four-year colleges and universities, or trade schools), **and I was accepted, but I do not plan on enrolling in the program right now**.
   e. I am **currently enrolled** at a college/university or trade school.
   f. I **received a college degree or professional license** in the past year.
   g. In the past year, **I have not thought about enrolling** in a college (including community college), university, or trade school.

If the respondent checks g, go to exit screen.
If the respondent checks a, b, c, d, e, or f, ask:

2. Have you applied for a MyCAA Scholarship to help pay for your education?

   Yes, I have **applied** for the scholarship, **but have not received it yet**.

   Yes, I have **received** the scholarship.

   No, I **did not know** about the scholarship.

No, I **am not eligible** for the scholarship.

No, I am waiting to **apply at a later date.**

No, I am in the process of **applying for the scholarship now.**

No, I **do not need/want** the scholarship.

No, I have not applied for the scholarship for another reason. (Please specify)

3. Have you used the MySECO website or asked your career counselor to help you explore or apply for other types of financial aid (for example, non–Department of Defense grants or scholarships, student loans)?

    Yes, these resources were **very helpful** with this process.

    Yes, these resources were **somewhat helpful** with this process.

    Yes, but these resources were **not at all helpful** with this process.

    No, I **have not used** these resources to help with this process, but I **have explored or applied** for other types of financial aid.

    No, I **have not explored** or applied for other types of financial aid.

4. Overall, how helpful has the MySECO website or your career counselor been in helping you **get the education or training** you need for your career?

    Very helpful

    Somewhat helpful

    Not at all helpful

5. Please indicate which of the following statements best applies to your current job situation (check one):

    – I am **not currently working** at a job, and I am **thinking about looking for a job.**

    – I am **not currently working** at a job, and I am **actively looking for a job.**

- I **am currently working** at a job, and I am **thinking about looking for a new job**.
- I **am currently working** at a job, and I am **actively looking for a new job**.
- I **am currently working** at a job, and I am **not looking for a new job**.
- I am **not currently working** at a job, and I am **not looking for a job**.

6. How many jobs have you applied for in the past month?

0

1–3

4–10

10–20

More than 20

If question 6 is any response greater than 0, ask:

6a. How many interviews did you get from those applications?

0

1–3

4–10

10–20

More than 20

6b. Have you applied for any jobs with companies who are MSEP corporate partners?

Yes, but I **have not interviewed** with any of these companies yet.

Yes, and **I have interviewed** with one or more of these companies.

No, I **have not applied** for any jobs **with companies who are MSEP corporate partners**.

I don't know.

7. Have you written or updated your resume since using the MySECO website or contacting your career counselor? (choose the option that best applies)

Yes, I wrote my resume after using the MySECO website or talking to my career counselor.

Yes, I updated or changed my existing resume after using the MySECO website or talking to my career counselor.

No, but I am planning on writing or updating my resume.

No, I am still thinking about my career options.

8. Have you ever had a state occupational license or certificate (for example, for a health care career, teaching, childcare, or accounting)?

Yes

No

If question 8 = Yes, ask:

8a.   Have you been able to successfully transfer your license or certificate when you've moved between states?

a. Yes, I have been able to transfer my license/certificate easily

b. Yes, I have been able to transfer my license/certificate, but it has been a hassle

c. No, I wanted to transfer my license/certificate, but was unable to

d. I have not moved from the state my license/certificate is in

e. I have not tried to transfer my license/certificate

If respondent checks 8a as a, b, or c, ask:

8b. How helpful was the MySECO website or your career counselor in helping you transfer your license/certificate to a new state?

Very helpful

Somewhat helpful

Not at all helpful

I did not use these resources

9. Did you use any SECO online support resources to connect with an MSEP mentor or search for jobs available from MSEP employer partners?

> Yes
>
> No

If question 9 = Yes, ask:

> 9a. How helpful was the online support resources in helping you connect with MSEP employers?
>
> > Very helpful
> > Somewhat helpful
> > Not at all helpful
> > I did not use these resources
>
> 9b. How would you rate your satisfaction with the variety of jobs available through MSEP partners?
>
> > Very: there is a wide variety
> > Somewhat: there is some variety
> > Not satisfied: there is no variety
> > I did not use these resources

10. Based on information from the MySECO website or your career counselor, are you thinking about changing the type of career you are interested in pursuing?

> Yes
>
> Somewhat
>
> No

11. Overall, how helpful has the MySECO website or your career counselor been in helping you choose a career field and/or helping you prepare to find a job?

> Very helpful
>
> Somewhat helpful
>
> Not at all helpful

RAND Suggested Questions for a MySECO Customer Feedback Questionnaire Follow-Up Questionnaire

An introductory script will explain the purpose of the questionnaire and request consent. As noted above, these questions would follow three to six months after the initial questionnaire.

1. Which of the following statements best applies to you? (check one)
   a. I have been **gathering information** about enrolling in a college (including community college), university, or trade school, **but I am not planning on applying to a program right now.**
   b. I have been **gathering information** about enrolling in a college (including community college), university, or trade school, **and I am planning on applying to a program this coming year.**
   c. I **have applied** to a degree or licensing program (including community colleges, 4-year colleges and universities, or trade schools), **but I have not been accepted yet.**
   d. I **applied** to a degree or licensing program (including community colleges, 4-year colleges and universities, or trade schools), **and I was accepted, but I do not plan on enrolling in the program right now.**
   e. I am **currently enrolled** at college/university or trade school.
   f. I **received a college degree or professional license** in the past year.
   g. In the past year, **I have not thought about enrolling** in a college (including community college), university, or trade school.

If Question 1 = g, go to exit screen.

If Question 1 = a, b, c, d, e, or f, ask:

2. Did you use the MySECO website or your career counselor help you choose a field of study, degree, or program to apply to?

    Yes, these resources were **very helpful** with my decision.

    Yes, these resources were **somewhat helpful** with my decision.

    Yes, but these resources were **not at all helpful** with my decision.

    No, I have not used these resources to help with my decision.

3. Have you applied for a My Career Advancement Account Scholarship to help pay for your education?

    Yes, I have **applied** for the scholarship, **but have not received it yet**.

    Yes, I have **received** the scholarship.

    No, I **did not know** about the scholarship.

    No, I **am not eligible** for the scholarship.

    No, I am waiting to **apply at a later date**.

    No, I am in the process of **applying for the scholarship now**.

    No, I **do not need/want** the scholarship.

    No, I have not applied for the scholarship for another reason. (Please specify)

If question 3 = "Yes, I have received the scholarship," ask:

    3a.   Have you used your My Career Advancement Account Scholarship to help pay for your education?

        Yes, and **I have used/am using the My Career Advancement Account Scholarship.**

        No, I **have not yet used the My Career Advancement Account Scholarship** to help pay for my education.

If 3a = "No...," ask:

> 3a1. Please specify why you haven't yet used your My Career Advancement Account Scholarship.

> 3b. Overall how helpful was the My Career Advancement Account Scholarship program (scholarship and counseling you received) in supporting your education and career objectives?
> Very helpful
> Somewhat helpful
> Not at all helpful

4. Have you used the MySECO website or your career counselor to help you explore or apply for other types of financial aid (for example, non–Department of Defense grants or scholarships, student loans)?

> Yes, these resources were **very helpful** with this process.
> Yes, these resources were **somewhat helpful** with this process.
> Yes, but these resources were **not at all helpful** with this process.
> No, I **have not used** these resources to help with this process but I **have explored or applied for** other types of financial aid.
> No, I **have not explored** or applied for other types of financial aid.

> 4a. How many other sources of financial aid have you used to pay for your education or training?
> 0
> 1
> 2
> 3
> 4
> 5
> More than 5

5. Overall, how helpful has the MySECO website or your career counselor been in helping you choose a career field and obtain the education or training you need for your career?
    Very helpful
    Somewhat helpful
    Not at all helpful

6. Please indicate which of the following statements best applies to your current job situation (check one):
    a. I am **not currently working** at a job, and I am **thinking about looking for a job.**
    b. I **am currently working** at a job, and I am **thinking about looking for a new job.**
    c. I am **not currently working** at a job, and I am **actively looking for a job.**
    d. I **am currently working** at a job, and I am **actively looking for a new job.**
    e. I am **not currently working** at a job, and I am **not looking for a job.**
    f. I **am currently working** at a job, and I am **not looking for a new job.**

If Question 6 = b, d, or f, ask:

6a. Which of the following best describes your current job (check one):
    I have a full-time job (more than 35 hours a week)
    I have a part-time job (less than 35 hours a week)
    I have more than one part-time jobs
    I have a seasonal or occasional job

6b. How much does your job make use of your skills, training, and/or experience?
    A great deal
    Somewhat
    Not at all

6c.   How satisfied are you with your current job?
A great deal
Somewhat
Not at all

6d.   How helpful were the resources available at the MySECO website or your career counselor in finding your job?
Very helpful
Somewhat helpful
Not at all helpful

6e.   Did you apply for any jobs with companies who are Military Spouse Employment Partnership corporate partners?
Yes
No
I don't know

6f.   Did you interview for any jobs with companies who are Military Spouse Employment Partnership corporate partners?
Yes
No
I don't know

6g.   Is your current job with an employer who is a Military Spouse Employment Partnership corporate partner?
Yes
No
I don't know

If Question 6 = a or c, ask:

7.   How many jobs have you applied for in the past 6 months?

0

1–3

4–10

10–20

More than 20

If question 7 is any response greater than 0, ask:

7a.   How many **interviews** did you get from those applications?

0

1–3

4–10

10–20

More than 20

7b.   How many **offers** did you get from those interviews or applications?

0

1–3

4–10

10–20

More than 20

7c.   Have you applied for any jobs with companies who are Military Spouse Employment Partnership corporate partners?

Yes, but I **have not interviewed** with any of these companies yet.

Yes, and **I have interviewed** with one or more of these companies.

No, I **have not applied for any jobs** yet.

No, I **have not applied** for any jobs **with companies who are Military Spouse Employment Partnership corporate partners**.

I don't know.

8. Have you ever had a state occupational license or certificate (for example, for a health care career, teaching, childcare, or accounting)?
    Yes
    No

If question 8 = Yes, ask:

    8a.   Have you been able to successfully transfer your license or certificate when you've moved between states?

      a. Yes, I have been able to transfer my license/certificate easily.

      b. Yes, I have been able to transfer my license/certificate, but it has been a hassle.

      c. No, I wanted to transfer my license/certificate, but was unable to.

      d. I have not moved from the state my license/certificate is in.

      e. I have not tried to transfer my license/certificate.

If 8a = a, b, or c, ask:

    8b.   How helpful was the MySECO website or your career counselor in helping you transfer your license/certificate to a new state?

      Very helpful
      Somewhat helpful
      Not at all helpful
      I did not use these resources

If question 6 = a, b, c, d, or f, ask:

9. Did you experience a move between states in the past six months?
    Yes
    No

If question 9 = Yes, ask:

    9a.   Did you need to request unemployment compensation upon arrival in the new state of residence?

      Yes
      No

If question 9a = Yes, ask:

> 9b. How satisfied were you with the process to obtain unemployment compensation?
> Very satisfied
> Somewhat satisfied
> Not at all satisfied

10. Overall, how helpful was the MySECO website or your career counselor in helping you choose a career field and/or helping you prepare to find a job?
    Very helpful
    Somewhat helpful
    Not at all helpful

References

Advisory Committee on Student Financial Assistance, *Pathways to Success: Integrating Learning with Life and Work to Increase National College Completion*, Washington, D.C.: U.S. Department of Education, February 2012. As of January 12, 2015:
http://www2.ed.gov/about/bdscomm/list/acsfa/ptsreport2.pdf

Bamberger, Michael, *RealWorld Evaluation*, Thousand Oaks, Calif.: Sage Publications, 2012.

Bamberger, Michael and Hewitt, Eleanor, *Monitoring and Evaluating Urban Development Programs, A Handbook for Program Managers and Researchers*. Washington, D.C., World Bank, Technical Paper No. 53, 1986.

Booth, Bradford, "Contextual Effects of Military Presence on Women's Earnings," *Armed Forces & Society*, Vol. 30, No. 1, 2003, pp. 25–51.

Booth, Bradford, William W. Falk, David R. Segal, and Mady Wechsler Segal, "The Impact of Military Presence in Local Labor Markets on the Employment of Women," *Gender & Society*, Vol. 14, No. 2, 2000, pp. 318–332.

Booth, Bradford, Mady Wechsler Segal, and D. Bruce Bell, *What We Know About Army Families: 2007 Update*, Fairfax, Va.: ICF International, 2007.

Bors, Phillip A., Allison Kemner, John Fulton, Jessica Stachecki, and Laura Brennan, "HKHC Community Dashboard: Design, Development, and Function of a Web-Based Performance Monitoring System," *Journal of Public Health Management Practice*, Vol. 21, No. 3 Supplement, 2015, pp. S36–S44.

Buryk, Peter, Thomas E. Trail, Gabriella Gonzalez, Laura L. Miller, and Esther M. Friedman, *Federal Educational Assistance Programs Available to Military Personnel: Program Design Features and Recommendations for Improved Delivery*, Santa Monica, Calif.: RAND Corporation, RR-664-OSD, 2015. As of April 28, 2016: http://www.rand.org/pubs/research_reports/RR664.html

Castaneda, Laura Werber, and Margaret C. Harrell, "Military Spouse Employment: A Grounded Theory Approach to Experiences and Perceptions," *Armed Forces & Society*, Vol. 34, No. 3, 2008, pp. 389–412.

Complete College America, *Time is the Enemy*, Washington, D.C., 2011. As of November 18, 2014:
http://www.completecollege.org/docs/Time_Is_the_Enemy_Summary.pdf

Cooke, Thomas J., and Karen Speirs, "Migration and Employment Among the Civilian Spouses of Military Personnel," *Social Science Quarterly*, Vol. 86, No. 2, 2005, pp. 343–355.

Cooney, Richard, *Moving with the Military: Race, Class and Gender Differences in the Employment Consequences of Tied Migration*, College Park, Md.: University of Maryland, dissertation, 2003.

Cooney, Richard, Karin De Angelis, and Mady W. Segal, "Moving with the Military: Race, Class, and Gender Differences in the Employment Consequences of Tied Migration," *Race, Gender and Class*, Vol. 18, No. 1–2, 2011, pp. 360–384.

Defense Manpower Data Center, *2012 Survey of Active Duty Spouses: Tabulations of Responses*, Alexandria, Va., 2013.

———, *2015 Survey of Active Duty Spouses: Tabulations of Responses*, Alexandria, Va., 2015.

DoD—*See* U.S. Department of Defense.

Doran, George T., "There's a S.M.A.R.T. Way to Write Management's Goals and Objectives," *Management Review*, Vol. 70, No. 11 (AMA FORUM), 1981, pp. 35–36.

Friedman, Esther M., Laura L. Miller, and Sarah Evans, *Advancing the Careers of Military Spouses: An Assessment of Education and Employment Goals and Barriers Facing Military Spouses Eligible for MyCAA*, Santa Monica, Calif.: RAND Corporation, RR-784-OSD, 2015. As of January 21, 2015:
http://www.rand.org/t/RR784.html

GAO—*See* U.S. Government Accountability Office.

Gonzalez, Gabriella C., Luke J. Matthews, Marek N. Posard, Parisa Roshan, and Shirley M. Ross, *Evaluation of the Military Spouse Employment Partnership: Progress Report on First Stage of Analysis*, Santa Monica, Calif.: RAND Corporation, RR-1349-OSD, 2015. As of April 28, 2016:
http://www.rand.org/pubs/research_reports/RR1349.html

Greenfield, Victoria A., Valerie L. Williams, Elisa Eiseman, *Using Logic Models for Strategic Planning and Evaluation: Application to the National Center for Injury Prevention and Control*, Santa Monica, Calif.: RAND Corporation, TR-370-NCIPC, 2006. As of April 28, 2016:
http://www.rand.org/pubs/technical_reports/TR370.html

Haims, Marla C., Melinda Moore, Harold D. Green, and Cynthia Clapp-Wincek, *Developing a Prototype Handbook for Monitoring and Evaluating Department of Defense Humanitarian Assistance Projects*, Santa Monica, Calif., RAND Corporation, TR-784-OSD, 2011. As of April 28, 2016: http://www.rand.org/pubs/technical_reports/TR784.html

Harkin, Thomas, *Benefitting Whom? For-Profit Education Companies and the Growth of Military Educational Benefits*, Washington, D.C.: U.S. Senate Health Education, Labor and Pensions Committee, December 8, 2010. As of March 15, 2016 (login required): http://www.nacacnet.org/issues-action/LegislativeNews/Documents/HELPMilEdReport.PDF

Harrell, Margaret, Nelson Lim, Laura Werber, and Daniela Golinelli, *Working Around the Military: Challenges to Military Spouse Employment and Education*, Santa Monica, Calif.: RAND Corporation, MG-196-OSD, 2004. As of April 28, 2016: http://www.rand.org/pubs/monographs/MG196.html

Heaton, Paul, and Heather Krull, *Unemployment Among Post-9/11 Veterans and Military Spouses After the Economic Downturn*, Santa Monica, Calif.: RAND Corporation, OP-376-OSD, 2012. As of April 28, 2016: http://www.rand.org/pubs/occasional_papers/OP376.html

Heaton, Paul, David S. Loughran, and Amalia Miller, *Compensating Wounded Warriors: An Analysis of Injury, Labor Market Earnings, and Disability Compensation Among Veterans of the Iraq and Afghanistan Wars*, Santa Monica, Calif.: RAND Corporation, MG-1166-OSD, 2012. As of April 28, 2016: http://www.rand.org/pubs/monographs/MG1166.html

Hisnanick, John, J., and Roger D. Little, "'Honey, I Love You, but . . .' Investigating the Causes of the Earnings Penalty of Being a Tied-Migrant Military Spouse," *Armed Forces & Society*, online January 10, 2014. As of July 23, 2014: http://afs.sagepub.com/content/early/2014/01/01/0095327X13512620

Ikemoto, Gina, and Julie Marsh, "Cutting Through the 'Data-Driven' Mantra: Different Conceptions of Data-Driven Decision Making," in Pamela Moss, ed., *Evidence and Decision Making*, Vol. 106, No. 1, National Society for the Study of Education Yearbook. 2007.

Jordan, Gretchen, "A Theory-Based Logic Model for Innovation Policy and Evaluation," *Research Evaluation*, Vol. 19, No. 4, 2010, pp. 263–274.

Kniskern, Mary K., and David R. Segal, *Mean Wage Differences Between Civilian and Military Wives*, University of Maryland: Center for Research on Military Organization, November 15, 2010.

Knowlton, Lisa Wyatt, and Cynthia C. Phillips, *The Logic Model Guidebook: Better Strategies for Great Results*, 2nd ed., Thousand Oaks, Calif.: Sage Publications, 2013.

Krapels, Joachim, Molly Morgan Jones, Sophie Castle-Clarke, David Kryl, and Obaid Younossi, *Developing a Research Impact Performance Management System for The Research Council, Oman: Final Report*, Santa Monica, Calif.: RAND Corporation, RR-833/1-TRC, 2015. As of December 8, 2015: http://www.rand.org/pubs/research_reports/RR833z1.html

Kusek, Jody Zall and Ray C. Rist, *Ten Steps to a Results-Based Monitoring and Evaluation System: A Handbook for Development Practitioners*, Washington, D.C.: World Bank, 2004.

Lim, Nelson, Daniela Golinelli, and Michelle Cho, *"Working Around the Military" Revisited: Spouse Employment in the 2000 Census Data*, Santa Monica, Calif.: RAND Corporation, MG-566-OSD, 2007. As of April 28, 2016: http://www.rand.org/pubs/monographs/MG566.html

Little, Roger D., and John J. Hisnanick, "The Earnings of Tied Migrant Military Husbands," *Armed Forces & Society*, Vol. 33, No. 4, 2007, pp. 547–570.

Marsh, Julie A., John F. Pane, and Laura S. Hamilton, *Making Sense of Data-Driven Decision Making in Education: Evidence from Recent RAND Research*, Santa Monica, Calif.: RAND Corporation, OP-170-EDU, 2006. As of April 28, 2016: http://www.rand.org/pubs/occasional_papers/OP170.html

McDavis, James C., and Laura R. L. Hawthorn, *Program Evaluation & Performance Measurement: An Introduction to Practice*, Thousand Oaks, Calif.: Sage Publications, 2006.

McLaughlin, John A., and Gretchen B. Jordan, "Logic Models: A Tool for Telling Your Program's Performance Story," *Evaluation and Program Planning*, Vol. 22, No. 1, 1999, pp. 65–72.

———, "Using Logic Models," in Joseph S. Wholey, Harry P. Hatry, and Kathryn E. Newcomer, eds., *Handbook of Practical Program Evaluation*, San Francisco: Jossey-Bass, 2010, pp. 7–32.

Military OneSource, *Legislative Best Practices for Military Spouse Unemployment Compensation*, undated. As of April 28, 2016: http://www.militaryonesource.mil/12038/USA4/Best%20Practices/ Unemployment%20Best%20Practices.pdf

Military Spouse Employment Partnership, *MSEP: Partner Commitments and Expectations*, February 2014. As of May 9, 2016: https://myseco.militaryonesource.mil/Portal/Media/Default/Collaterals_Catalog/ Career_Connections/MSEP-Partner-Commitments-and-Expectations.pdf

Military Spouse Employment Partnership Career Portal, homepage, undated-a. As of April 28, 2016: https://msepjobs.militaryonesource.mil/msep/

———, "All Partners," web page, undated-b. As of January 6, 2015: https://msepjobs.militaryonesource.mil/partners/all

Needels, Karen, and Heather Hesketh Zaveri, *Additional Findings from the Military Spouse Career Advancement Accounts Demonstration: Implementation Progress and Participants' Characteristics and Plans*, Princeton, N.J.: Mathematica Policy Research, Inc., 2009.

Office of the Deputy Assistant Secretary of Defense for Military Community and Family Policy, *2013 Demographics: Profile of the Military Community*, Washington, D.C., 2014.

Office of the Deputy Under Secretary of Defense, *Report on Military Spouse Education and Employment*, Washington, D.C.: Military Community and Family Policy, January 2008.

OMB—*See* U.S. Office of Management and Budget.

Patton, Michael Q., *Utilization-Focused Evaluation*, 4th ed., Thousand Oaks, CA: Sage Publications, 2008.

Public Law 103-62, Government Performance and Results Act, 1993. As of December 9, 2015:
http://www.whitehouse.gov/omb/mgmt-gpra/gplaw2m

Public Law 111-352, Government Performance and Results Act Modernization Act, 2010. As of December 9, 2015:
http://www.gpo.gov/fdsys/pkg/PLAW-111publ352/pdf/PLAW-111publ352.pdf

Reed, John H., and Gretchen Jordan, "Using Systems Theory and Logic Models to Define Integrated Outcomes and Performance Measures in Multi-Program Settings," *Research Evaluation*, Vol. 16, No. 3, 2007, pp. 169–181.

Riemer, Manuel, and Leonard Bickman, "Using Program Theory to Link Social Psychology and Program Evaluation," in Melvin M. Mark, Stewart I. Donaldson, and Bernadette Campbell, eds., *Social Psychology and Evaluation*, New York: Guilford Press, 2011.

Rossi, Peter H., Mark W. Lipsey, and Howard E. Freeman, *Evaluation: A Systematic Approach*, Thousand Oaks, Calif.: Sage Publications, 2004.

Ryan, Gery W., Evan Bloom, David Lowsky, Mark T. Linthicum, Timothy Juday, Lisa Rosenblatt, Sonali P. Kulkarni, Dana P. Goldman, and Jennifer N. Sayles, "Data-Driven Decision-Making Tools to Improve Public Resource Allocation for Care and Prevention of HIV/AIDS," *Health Affairs*, Vol. 33, No. 3, March 2014, pp. 410–417.

SECO—*See* Spouse Education and Career Opportunities.

Spouse Education and Career Opportunities, "Career Search," 2016. As of May 10, 2016:
https://aiportal.acc.af.mil/mycaa/Career/Search.aspx

Swan, Gerry, "Tools for Data-Driven Decision Making in Teacher Education," *Journal of Computing in Teacher Education*, Vol. 25, No. 3, 2009, pp. 107–113.

United Nations Evaluation Group (UNEG), *Norms for Evaluation in the UN System*, Washington, D.C.: United Nations, April 2005. As of December 17, 2014: http://www.unevaluation.org/document/detail/21

U.S. Agency for International Development, *Glossary of Evaluation Terms*, Washington, D.C.: Planning and Performance Management Unit, Office of the Director of Foreign Assistance, March 25, 2009.

U.S. Agency for International Development and Social Impact, Inc., *Performance Management Plan (PMP) Toolkit: A Guide for Missions on Planning for, Developing, Updating, and Actively Using a PMP*, Office of Learning, Evaluation and Research, Bureau of Policy, Planning and Learning (PPL/LER), October, 2013.

U.S. Department of Defense, *Military Family Readiness*, Washington, D.C., DoD Instruction 1342.22, July 3, 2012. As of November 20, 2014: http://www.dtic.mil/whs/directives/corres/pdf/134222p.pdf

U.S. Department of the Treasury and Department of Defense, *Support Our Military Families: Best Practices for Streamlining Occupational Licensing Across State Lines*, Washington, D.C., February 2012.

U.S. Government Accountability Office, *Performance Measurement and Evaluation*, Washington, D.C., GAO-11-646SP, 2011. As of December 9, 2015: http://www.gao.gov/products/GAO-11-646SP

———, *Military Spouse Employment Programs: DoD Can Improve Guidance and Performance Monitoring*, Washington, D.C., 2012. As of January 28, 2015: http://gao.gov/assets/660/650867.pdf

U.S. Office of Management and Budget, *Fiscal Year 2014: Analytic Perspectives, Budget of the U.S. Government*, Washington, D.C.: Office of Management and Budget, 2013. As of December 9, 2015: http://www.whitehouse.gov/omb/budget/Analytical_Perspectives/

USA4MilitaryFamilies, "Issue Seven: Removing Licensure Impediments for Transitioning Military Spouses," web page, May 14, 2016. As of May 10, 2016: http://www.usa4militaryfamilies.dod.mil/MOS/f?p=USA4:ISSUE:0::::P2_ISSUE:7

White House, *Strengthening Our Military Families: Meeting America's Commitment*, Washington, D.C., 2011. As of February 23, 2016: http://permanent.access.gpo.gov/gpo6289/Strengthening_our_Military_January_2011.pdf

Wholey, Joseph S., Harry P. Hatry, and Kathryn E. Newcomer, eds., *Handbook of Practical Program Evaluation*, Vol. 19, San Francisco: Jossey-Bass, 2010.

Williams, Valerie L., Elisa Eiseman, Eric Landree, and David M. Adamson, *Demonstrating and Communicating Research Impact: Preparing NIOSH Programs for External Review*, Santa Monica, Calif.: RAND Corporation, MG-809-NIOSH, 2009. As of November 19, 2015:
http://www.rand.org/pubs/monographs/MG809.html

W. K. Kellogg Foundation, *Using Logic Models to Bring Together Planning, Evaluation, and Action: Logic Model Development Guide*, Battle Creek, Mich., 2004. As of November 18, 2014:
https://www.wkkf.org/resource-directory/resource/2006/02/wk-kellogg-foundation-logic-model-development-guide

World Bank, *An Overview of Monitoring and Evaluation in the World Bank.* Operations Evaluation Department Report No. 13247, Washington, D.C., 1994.

World Bank Operations Evaluation Department, *Designing Project Monitoring and Evaluation*, Lessons and Practices, No 8, June 1996.

Zaveri, Heather Hesketh, Caterina Pisciotta, and Linda Rosenberg, *The Implementation Evaluation of the Military Spouse Career Advancement Accounts Demonstration (2009): Part I: Early Implementation of the Military Spouse Career Advancement Accounts Demonstration*, Princeton, N.J.: Mathematica Policy Research, Inc., 2009.